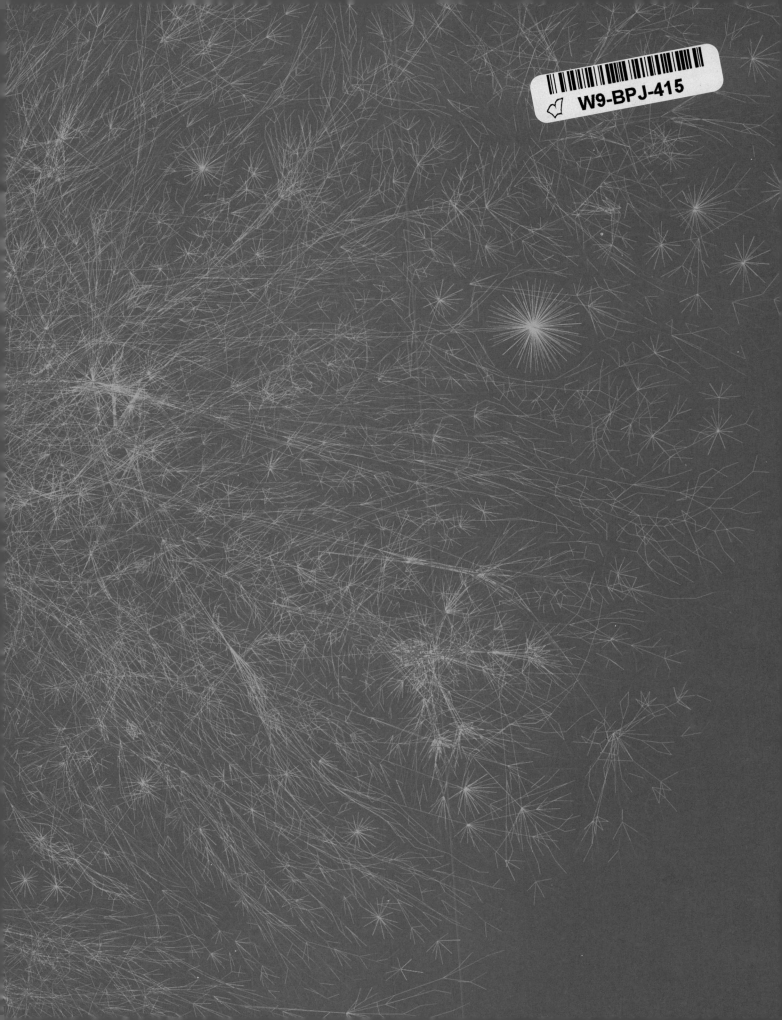

CHILDREN'S
COOL
TECHNOLOGY
ENCYCLOPEDIA

Author: Steve Parker
Consultant: Adam Nieman

This edition produced by Tall Tree Ltd, London

First published by Parragon in 2008
Parragon
Queen Street House
4 Queen Street
Bath BA1 1HE, UK

ISBN 978-1-4075-1316-4

Printed in Indonesia

CHILDREN'S COOL TECHNOLOGY ENCYCLOPEDIA

STEVE PARKER

Bath · New York · Singapore · Hong Kong · Cologne · Delhi · Melbourne

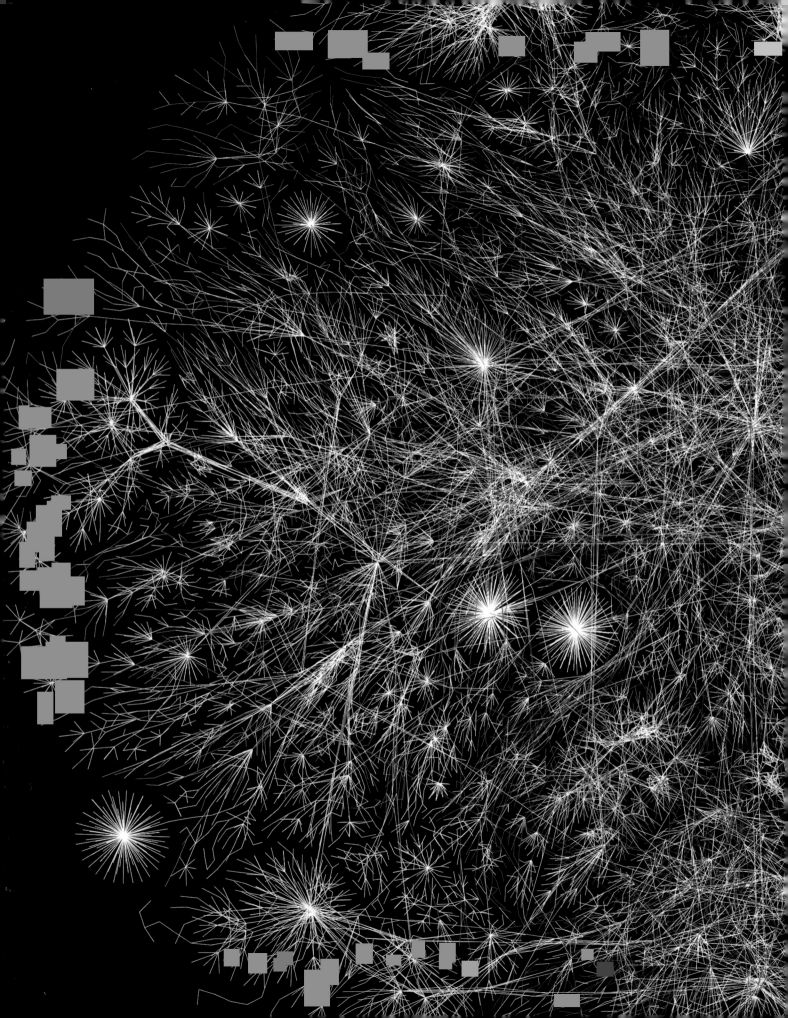

CONTENTS

GAMES CONSOLES

INTRODUCTION INTRO

SMART CARD

NANOTECH

SPEECH

INTRODUCTION

Not so long ago, a cell phone was the size of a brick, and the music on your MP3 player would have filled shelves with old vinyl discs. The times are changing fast. Today, we are experiencing a revolution in technology. Every week, smarter gadgets, more advanced medicines, and more powerful computers become part of daily life. Modern machines can think with microchips smaller than this period. They can be superlight and ultra-tough, built with advanced metal composites. They need no trailing wires, because they have Wi-Fi radio links. Progress seems unstoppable. But technology can also overwhelm us. How do the latest widgets work? Which of tomorrow's breakthroughs should we be ready for? And who's in charge— us or the machines? Find out inside. This book has the know-how on the latest, coolest technology out there.

FUN

GAMES CONSOLES 12-13

MP3 PLAYER 10-11

Stone Age people had no MP3 players, computer games, or wide-screen TVs. What on earth did they do with their lives? Today, an incredible array of hi-tech gadgets lets us escape from real life and daily routine into a fantastic world of sights, sounds, and action. We can battle against imaginary monsters, fulfill quests, and find treasure, or just sit back and listen to our favorite tracks—from gadgets that fit into the palms of our hands.

< 08 >

VIRTUAL WORLD 26-27

iPod
Music	>
Photos	>
Extras	>
Settings	>
Shuffle Songs	
Backlight	

MENU

MP3 PLAYER

Only a few years ago, music on the move meant a large, portable CD player—and if it got jogged it sk-sk-skipped. Now "flash" memory devices mean hours of skip-free portable tunes can be stored in a gadget as small as a finger.

Stroke the clickwheel to select on-screen menus.

The USB attachment plugs into a computer.

The iPod, first released in 2001, is Apple's version of an MP3 (short for Mpeg 1, Audio Layer 3) player. It must be used with Apple's music application (program), iTunes.

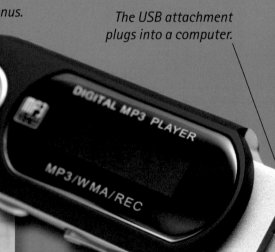

DIGITAL MP3 PLAYER
MP3/WMA/REC

DOWNLOADING MUSIC

MP3

An online music store

Music is usually transferred to an MP3 player from a computer. To get the songs into the computer, they are ripped from a compact disc (CD) or similar source into a compressed audio format, the most common of which is MP3. They can also be downloaded onto the computer from a music store on the Internet.

FLASH VS. DISC

Sounds are stored by MP3 players in two main ways. One is the flash drive, which is a memory microchip with no moving parts. The other is a tiny hard-disc drive, like the spinning magnetic disc in a computer's hard drive. Flash drives are smaller, lighter, use less power, and do not skip if banged. Hard drives store much more—thousands of songs, photographs, or movies—but the moving part makes them less durable. One gigabyte (GB) of memory holds roughly 250 songs.

Surfers, kitesurfers, and snowboarders say that listening to music on a waterproof MP3 player helps get them in the right mood before competitions.

MP4 WATCHES

These store music, video, photos, games, and other information downloaded from a computer in the MP4 (audio and video) format. The watch has a flash memory, a small screen, and plug-in headphones. Some can record sounds. They also tell the time!

Side buttons for control

The display shows a clock face when "resting."

The dock may be battery powered or run on household electricity.

An MP3 dock (docking station) has a slot to plug in the player, which feeds the music into a powerful amplifier and loudspeakers. The MP3 player charges its battery while docked.

The remote control copies some functions of the MP3 player's control system.

GAMES CONSOLES

When you play a video game, you enter into a world of make-believe through a games console. This is an interactive entertainment computer connected to a video display. All *you* need is quick thinking—and fast fingers!

The Xbox 360 is a "7th generation" system from Microsoft. You can use it to play against others on the Internet.

GAME GRAPHICS

Every year computer graphics and animation are clearer, faster moving, and more realistic. The first two-dimensional computer games were slow and jerky; today's games place you in an interactive three-dimensional world. Details, such as moving shadows and reflecting light, are added to make the graphics more real.

Pop-up panels appear in a flash.

Characters are made from three-dimensional shapes called polygons.

Computer game for 8 to 12 year olds

CD and DVD tray

The games controller can be linked wirelessly using radio signals.

XBOX 360

Nintendo's DS Lite ("DS" is for "dual screen") has one ordinary screen and a touch-screen one. A wireless link allows you to play with others nearby.

The console is lightweight and foldaway.

MAKING GAMES

Making a computer game can take a team of people up to three years. Graphic designers decide on the look of the scenes, the colors, characters, and backgrounds. Animators work out how objects move, appear, enlarge, or shrink. Strategists decide on the game's rules. Software specialists convert all this information into a language the computer understands.

One of Nintendo's most successful games is Donkey Kong, featuring a giant gorilla. He first appeared in 1981 and has had four makeovers since.

MINI GAMES

In the fast-growing world of mini games, you can play a simple game just to fill a few minutes, while you're on a bus, bored, or waiting on a line. Mini games need little memory and have simple controls. They can be played on cell phones, MP4 watches, MP3 players, and handheld portable games consoles.

Relatively basic graphics

These mini games can be downloaded from the Internet.

Wii

The Wii, launched in 2006, is the fifth home games console from Nintendo. Its coolest feature is the handheld Wii Remote (nicknamed Wiimote), a wireless controller that can sense motion and rotation. The Wii can also connect to the Internet.

The Wii is Nintendo's smallest console, at 1¾ inches (44 mm) wide, 6 inches (157 mm) tall, and 8½ inches (215 mm) deep—about the size of three DVD cases side by side. Its media drive slot accepts older game discs.

ON-SCREEN ACTION

The on-screen batter makes your hit.

In the Wii version of baseball, the player steps up to the plate and whacks the baseball as hard as he or she can using the Wiimote as a bat. From the console's rumble function and speaker comes the thunderous roar of the crowd. The player can also swing the Wiimote to pitch to the batter. Playing with a team of friends adds to the fun.

The Wiimote is easy to use and is designed to appeal to grown-ups and kids alike. It also contains a speaker that makes sound effects as the player strikes an object.

ACCESSORIES

There are a number of accessories that make the Wii gaming experience even more realistic. These include a steering wheel, which comes with such games as *Monster 4x4 World Circuit*, plus swords, knives, gloves, and a sports pack that contains a tennis racket and a golf club. The Wiimote slots into each one of these handheld accessories and visualizes the player's action on screen.

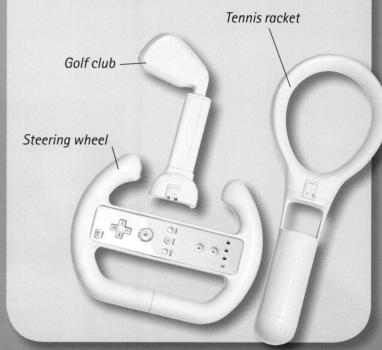

Tennis racket

Golf club

Steering wheel

HOW IT WORKS

The Wiimote is a revolutionary controller that can sense its position in three-dimensional space. This is because it contains devices called accelerometers, which detect acceleration, or movement, in three dimensions as you wave it around. The Wiimote is connected to the console wirelessly. A wrist strap prevents the player from accidentally throwing the Wiimote across the room in the heat of the action!

DIGITAL CAMERA

With a traditional film camera, you have an annoying wait of days before you see your photos printed. With a digital camera, you can check the images on the camera's screen right after shooting, dump the dud ones, and make printed photos minutes later.

The Canon Ixus is a pocket-size camera with a zoom lens. The photos it takes are each seven megapixels (MP)—one MP is a million pixels in size.

HOW MANY PIXELS?

"Pixel" is short for "picture element." A pixel is one tiny part of an image. An image is made up of many pixels, each with its own color and brightness. The number of pixels in a certain area is called the resolution. Higher resolution means more, smaller pixels, which makes the image sharper and more detailed.

1 pixel

The camera's memory card stores the photos electronically on a set of microchips.

Here, a pixel is pulled out as an individual block of color. Resolution is measured by the number of pixels in each inch of the image.

The camera casing contains and protects the lens, memory card, rechargeable battery, CCD chip, and a microprocessor that analyzes the image for its correct exposure.

Light sensor

The lens focuses light rays onto the CCD.

The flash activates if light levels are too low.

LIGHT WORK

Inside a digital camera, light from the scene shines onto a microchip called a charge-coupled device (CCD). This has millions of tiny pixels. Each pixel senses the brightness and color of the light ray hitting it, and converts it to an electronic signal. All the signals from all the pixels make up a version of the scene in electronic form, which is stored in the camera's memory card.

MAKING PRINTS

The data from the memory card is sent to a printer. This converts each pixel of the picture into a spot of ink of a particular color and brightness. Thousands of spots close together form the whole image.

Printer transfer cable

Photo paper tray

CANON ZOOM LENS 3x 5.8-17.4mm 1:2.8-4.9

7.1 MEGA PIXELS

A single lens reflex (SLR) camera has a camera body plus various lenses, such as wide angle to fit in a big scene or telephoto to bring distant subjects nearer.

DIGITAL CAMCORDER

Birthdays, vacations, ceremonies, new baby, accidentally falling flat on your face—they can all be captured forever on home video by the camcorder, a combined camera-recorder for pictures and sounds.

The camcorder fits neatly into a cupped hand so that all the main buttons and switches, such as record and zoom, are at the user's fingertips.

The zoom lens enlarges the central scene, allowing you to see the action in close-up.

FUJINON ZOOM LENS

10x OPTICAL f=3.3~33mm 1:1.8 Ø46

FOCUS

FOCUS ASSIST

DIGITAL BROADCASTING

Digital television and digital radio (known as DAB— digital audio broadcasting), use fast, on-off pulses of radio waves. The on-off pulses represent the 0s and 1s of digital code, which are converted by the television into images and sounds. Digital signals give better quality pictures and sounds compared with non-digital broadcasts. They also pack more channels into the same range of radio waves.

Digital video enables TV sports programs to provide faster replays and interactive elements, such as different camera angles.

LINKS ‹ 16 DIGITAL CAMERA

The eyepiece hood keeps out light for a clear view of the scene.

A rotating fold-out screen provides instant viewing.

DIGITAL EDITING

Home video editing program

Video editing programs, such as *Final Cut Pro*, let the user select and combine audio and video segments in order to tell an interesting story. These programs allow the footage to be broken up into individual frames. You can edit to make a sudden change or fade from one view into another.

Extra controls are hidden under the fold-out tilting screen, which shows menus and choices, as well as the scenes recorded.

SHARPER, CLEARER

The 3CCD camcorder has three microchips called charge-coupled devices (CCDs). Each one has many tiny pixels that are sensitive to only one of three colors: red, green, or blue. For example, the red CCD detects the brightness of red light rays falling on each of its pixels and converts them to electronic signals. The result is three complete sets of signals, one for each color. These can be fed to the red, green, and blue spots in the pixels of a television screen for more realistic colors.

CD, DVD, HVD

Discs are everywhere! Compact discs (CDs) were invented in 1979 and are mostly used for storing music. Then came the digital versatile disc (DVD), with enough storage for a full-length movie. Next is the holographic versatile disc (HVD)—it can store up to 100 movies!

The disc sits in a sliding tray.

PITS AND FLATS

CDs and DVDs are optical discs—that means they are "read" using a laser beam. Their surface has millions of micro-pits. A laser beam reflects differently off the pits and flats between, and these reflections are turned into digital information by a sensor. DVDs can store more information than CDs.

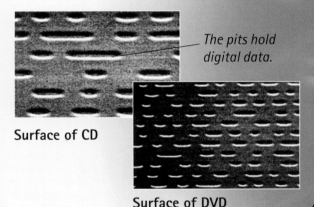

The pits hold digital data.

Surface of CD

Surface of DVD

Laser

The laser beam aims at the disc's shiny underside and starts reading from the center. The disc's spin rate becomes slower as the beam moves outward so that the pits and flats pass at a constant speed.

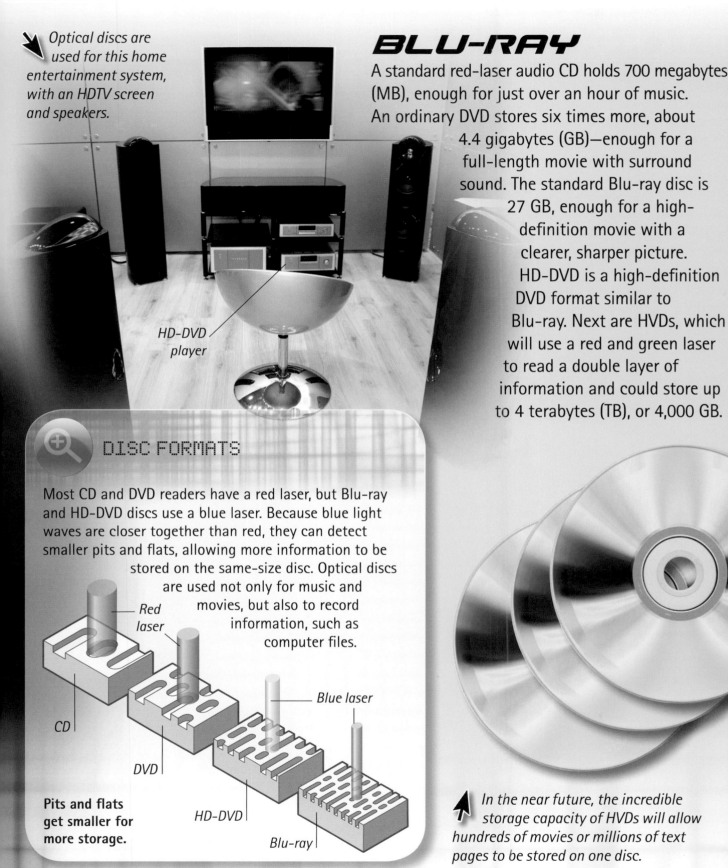

Optical discs are used for this home entertainment system, with an HDTV screen and speakers.

HD-DVD player

BLU-RAY

A standard red-laser audio CD holds 700 megabytes (MB), enough for just over an hour of music. An ordinary DVD stores six times more, about 4.4 gigabytes (GB)—enough for a full-length movie with surround sound. The standard Blu-ray disc is 27 GB, enough for a high-definition movie with a clearer, sharper picture. HD-DVD is a high-definition DVD format similar to Blu-ray. Next are HVDs, which will use a red and green laser to read a double layer of information and could store up to 4 terabytes (TB), or 4,000 GB.

DISC FORMATS

Most CD and DVD readers have a red laser, but Blu-ray and HD-DVD discs use a blue laser. Because blue light waves are closer together than red, they can detect smaller pits and flats, allowing more information to be stored on the same-size disc. Optical discs are used not only for music and movies, but also to record information, such as computer files.

Red laser

Blue laser

CD

DVD

HD-DVD

Blu-ray

Pits and flats get smaller for more storage.

In the near future, the incredible storage capacity of HVDs will allow hundreds of movies or millions of text pages to be stored on one disc.

MICROCHIP

Microchips are the "brains" of almost every smart gadget and electronic device. They are tiny, thin wafers—"chips"—of the substance silicon, containing thousands or even millions of microscopic components.

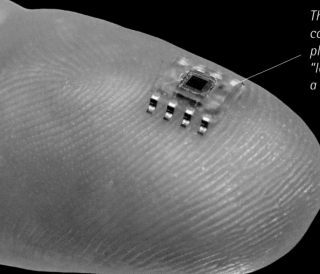

This microchip is contained in a clear plastic case. Its metal "legs" connect it into a larger circuit.

MAKING CHIPS

A chip's components are created on top of the silicon wafer in various ways. They can be burned into different layers of the chip with ultraviolet light, a laser, or strong acid chemicals. The components are made in position and connected, or integrated, so microchips are also called integrated circuits (ICs).

Once integrated, the chip is protected inside a much larger plastic casing.

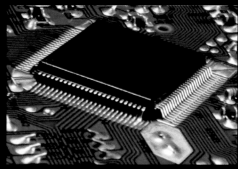

CHIPS ONBOARD

Microchips are designed on huge boards with the help of other microchips—those in computers. They are then connected into a circuit board. A typical home computer has 20 or more chips on its main circuit board (the motherboard).

ESSENTIAL FOR > cell phone · digital camera · games console · smart card

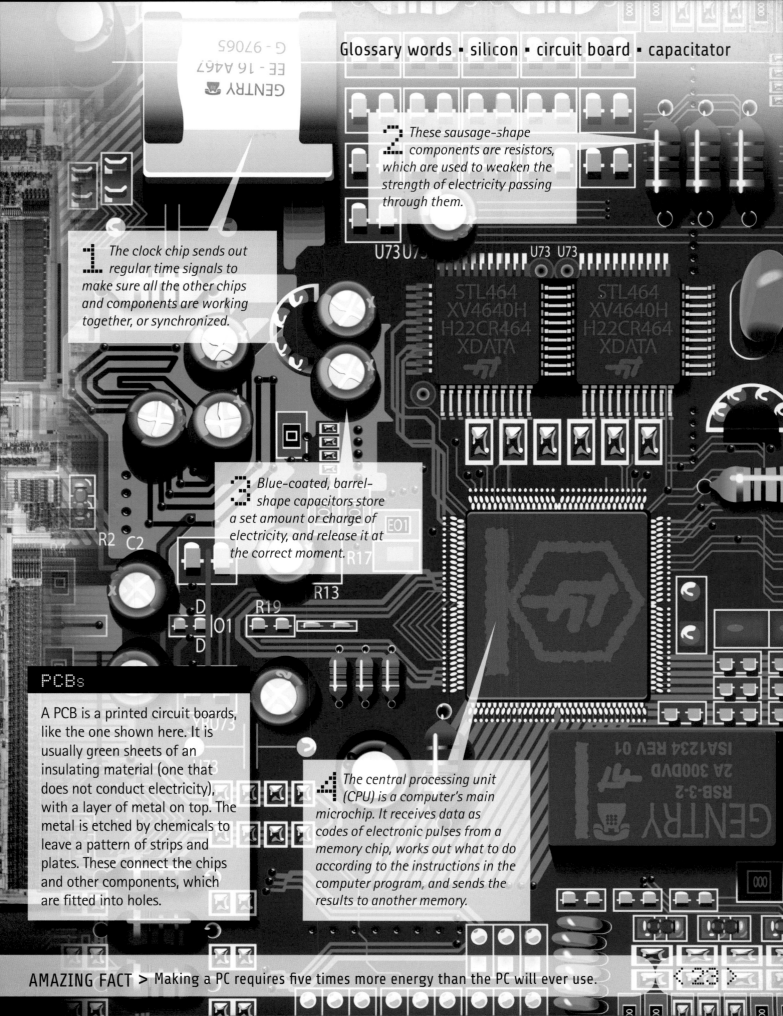

GENTRY
EE - 16 A467
G - 97065

2 These sausage-shape components are resistors, which are used to weaken the strength of electricity passing through them.

1 The clock chip sends out regular time signals to make sure all the other chips and components are working together, or synchronized.

STL464
XV4640H
H22CR464
XDATA

STL464
XV4640H
H22CR464
XDATA

U73 U73

U73 U73

3 Blue-coated, barrel-shape capacitors store a set amount or charge of electricity, and release it at the correct moment.

EO1

R2 C2

R17

R13

D
01
D

R19

PCBs

A PCB is a printed circuit boards, like the one shown here. It is usually green sheets of an insulating material (one that does not conduct electricity), with a layer of metal on top. The metal is etched by chemicals to leave a pattern of strips and plates. These connect the chips and other components, which are fitted into holes.

4 The central processing unit (CPU) is a computer's main microchip. It receives data as codes of electronic pulses from a memory chip, works out what to do according to the instructions in the computer program, and sends the results to another memory.

ISA1234 REV 01
2A 300DVD
RSB-3.2
GENTRY

000

WIDE SCREEN

Televisions are no longer ugly, bulky boxes. Today's sleek, flat, wide-screen panels can hang on the wall. The two main television technologies are liquid crystal display (LCD) and plasma.

A flat screen reflects less light.

LCD TELEVISION

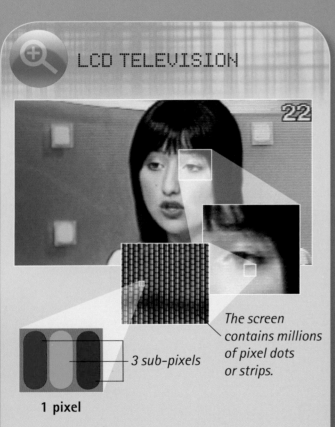

22

The screen contains millions of pixel dots or strips.

3 sub-pixels

1 pixel

An LCD screen contains millions of tiny semiliquid crystals or pixels. Each has three sub-pixels of red, green, and blue—the primary colors of light. Different combinations and brightness make up the other colors. When all three shine together they look white. These crystals "twist" when electricity passes through them to let through different amounts of light.

Most flat wide-screen televisions use thin film transistor (TFT) technology. In TFT, one transistor controls just one pixel. This allows the screen image to "refresh" itself many times a second, which reduces flickering.

The stand positions the TV for correct viewing and houses the wiring.

Speakers on either side of the screen produce stereo sound.

A flat screen can be hung on the wall like a painting.

4:3

16:9 (Wide screen)

Old cathode ray tube (CRT) TVs have screen proportions of 4 units wide to 3 high, or 4:3. Wide screen is usually 16:9, which better fills the field of vision that our eyes naturally see.

PLASMA SCREEN

Plasma screens also have pixels, like LCDs, but each pixel is made up of three tiny boxlike cells containing a special gas. When electricity passes through, the gas turns into plasma and glows bright red, blue, or green. Controlling the electrical signals alters the brightness and color combinations. Many still images flash up every second, one after the other, and the eye merges them into a smooth, continuous movement.

HIGH DEFINITION

High-definition television (HDTV) means the screen contains more, and tinier, pixels. This makes small details of the picture clearer. Also, each time HDTV shows a split-second image, the image covers the whole screen. In older televisions, different areas of the screen show their parts of the image at slightly different times, which causes flickering.

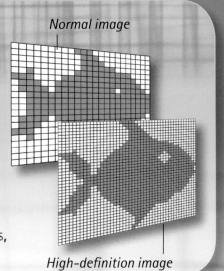

Normal image

High-definition image

VIRTUAL WORLD

In a virtual world, you can lead armies, build cities, and adopt any persona you like. Some worlds are games with objectives. Others, such as *Second Life*, are online universes where you can interact with other users.

City Life, *released in 2006, is the first game where you can build a city in full three dimensions You can move sideways, to and fro, and zoom in close almost anywhere. Its follow-up is* Cities Unlimited.

Buildings do not have to follow a grid plan as in previous city games.

Complex structures, such as bridges, can be built.

VIRTUAL WORLD BEHAVIOR

An arsonist strikes the City's downtown.

Most virtual worlds have their own rules to ensure that users are treated fairly. If you break them, you might get thrown out. For example, there are rules that say you must not assault anyone, pester players who do not want to talk to you, reveal private information about other players, or advertise real-world products in the virtual world.

Each city in City Life *is populated by thousands of computer-generated citizens, divided into various groups. The challenge is to organize the city so that these groups can live together peacefully.*

SIM CITIES

With sim (simulation) city games you can establish an entire city—with power stations, factories, highways, streets, stores, parks, entertainment facilities, and people—all to your own design. The city layout is stored in your computer's memory so you can move around it and see different places, but the game's creators make sure that there are always challenges for the gamer— for example, some of the workers may go on strike or riot, or a thunderstorm might cause power outages and flood the streets.

CREATING AN AVATAR

"Avatar" is an old word meaning a god in human or animal form. It has also come to mean a character in the virtual world—a person, animal, monster, spirit, or even a symbol. People create the appearance, style, personality, behavior, and reactions of their own avatars to represent them in games and online chat rooms. In the virtual world, you really can be anyone you want to be.

Avatars can have complex movements and expressions.

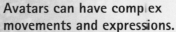

CLUB SOUNDS

It's getting late, and you want to shake your stuff on the dance floor. Welcome to the world of clubbing, where DJs play tracks on hi-tech decks. Mixing tracks requires skill and timing. Recording the tracks in a modern digital studio requires sophisticated technology.

A DJ controls what people hear through the sound system. He or she must always be one step ahead, preparing to drop in the next tracks so that the beats mix in and the change is barely noticeable. Cushioned headphones keep out the noise of the club and help the DJ to switch between tracks.

Twin decks, one for each hand

A keyboard is linked to a monitor for playing samples or tracks from the DJ's computer.

Cup headphones

MIXING DECK

The controls fade in sounds and alter the speed of the decks.

A DJ uses a real or virtual deck (controlled from a laptop) to mix one track into another, using headphones to "drop" a second track over the beat of the first. A good DJ can also use the deck to "scratch" (repeat a beat or musical phrase) and speed up or slow down the track to make it match the preceding one.

RECORDING

Digital studios record sounds onto a computer's hard disc. Microphones are used to record acoustic instruments that make their own sounds, such as piano, drums, and guitar. Electronic instruments, such as a synthesizer, can be fed straight into a mixing desk. Each sound is recorded separately and the individual tracks are mixed together to create the final track. A producer can enhance the recording with studio tricks, such as multitracking, where a voice or instrument can be recorded over itself to give a "thicker" sound.

 STUDIO MIXING

The mixing desk has a set of controls for each separate instrument.

The studio mixing desk has many sets of sliders and dials. There is one set for each track, which is a recording of one instrument. The controls adjust the sound of the instrument—for example, by altering its balance of high and low tones (known as equalization, or EQ). The separate tracks are then merged together and their individual volumes carefully altered to make the final combined recording, which is known as the master track.

Mixing programs show the sounds as spiky waves, or sonograms.

< 29 >

BIG-SCREEN VIDEO

Huge video screens can be used to show news, advertisements, and action replays. Using the same principle as television screens, the fast-changing still pictures appear to be in continuous motion.

These screens in downtown Tokyo, Japan carry animated advertising. They can switch in an instant to display news stories, or warnings of earthquakes or approaching storms.

Big-screen LEDs are bright enough to be seen even in strong sunlight.

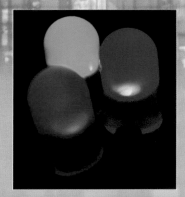

PIXEL LED

Big screens, like small ones, are made up of small units called pixels, each with three colors (red, blue, and green). On a really big screen, these colors are created by thumb-sized light-emitting diodes (LEDs). From far away, the eyes merge the separate pixels created from these LEDs into areas of smooth color.

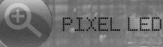

Each pixel has three LEDs.

Light is emitted by passing a current through a semiconductor, such as diamond.

Contact wires connect to the power source.

 Animation on a big LED screen forms a backdrop to a movie premiere in Leicester Square, London. Here, the action is run across multiple screens.

ANIMATION

Computer-generated images (CGI) are created using highly sophisticated software. Initial sketches of the object are built up into highly detailed images using the computer program. This creates a three-dimenional "map" of the object, letting the animator twist, turn, and move it in any direction. After the animator creates the start and finish positions for the object, the computer can calculate all the positions in between so that it appears to move smoothly.

IMAX CINEMA

"Image Maximum," or IMAX, cinemas give a unique cinematic experience. The massive 52½-feet (16-m) high screen covers almost the entire field of vision. IMAX movies are shot on special film that is ten times larger than normal film, giving it a much higher resolution. In order to expose at the standard film speed of 24 frames per second, however, the film must move three times faster through the camera.

IMAX screens, such as this one in London, England, show specially shot films, including some in three dimensions.

— *This LED screen at the Razorback Stadium, Arkansas, also carries score information.*

Video cameras take close-up pictures of stage performers, which are shown instantly on the LED screen. This gives a close-up view to people 650 feet (200 m) away at the back of the stadium.

ROLLER COASTER

After a hard day playing computer games, it's time for the real deal—getting spun around and flung upside down on a roller coaster. Bigger, faster coasters open every year around the world, each bidding to be the most thrilling ride of all.

HI-TECH STRUCTURES

A modern roller coaster is designed to withstand enormous forces as cars full of people hurtle around bends and loops at high speed. It also has to resist high winds and bad weather. Kingda Ka in New Jersey is the world's tallest, fastest roller coaster, with a vertical track that's three times taller than the Statue of Liberty. Its cars reach a speed of 128 miles per hour.

Kingda Ka in New Jersey, opened in 2005.

The tubular track is very strong for its weight.

Corkscrews spin the cars up and over as they travel along and downward. The riders are kept in by body harnesses or restraints that go over the shoulders and around the waist.

As the view twists and turns, some riders have trouble knowing which way up they are. They may feel sick, but the adrenalin soon overcomes that.

Tubular towers support the track and also allow emergency access.

FORCES

Some roller coasters pull the cars to the highest part of the track, using teeth on the car's underside that lock into a moving chain. Others have hydraulic pistons, using oil under great pressure to shoot the car to a speed of 125 miles per hour in less than four seconds! After this, the track goes up and down and around, but gradually its average height gets lower. In this way, the force of gravity pulls the cars downward and keeps them rolling.

MECHANISM

The upstop wheels secure seats to the structure.

Many roller coaster cars have two sets of wheels. The main set takes the car's weight when it's upright on the track. The other set, called upstop wheels, runs above the track rails and stops the car flying off as it banks, loops, and rolls. At the top of a hill, the momentum in the riders' bodies wants to continue going upward, so riders feel as if they're floating and weightless—an experience known as "airtime."

STAY CONNECTED

BLACKBERRY 42-43

Ever since shepherds first yodeled to each other across the valleys, people have devised new ways of communicating across longer and longer distances. The first electric form of communication was the telegraph in the 1830s, which used a dot-dash code. From the 1870s speech was possible over telephone wires. Cell phones using radio-wave links first appeared in the 1980s. Today, there are dozens of wireless ways to keep in touch from anywhere in the world.

WEBCAM 40-41

CELL PHONE

How did people *ever* live without cell phones? The modern cell phone may not be shrinking in size any more, but its growing list of features includes camera, video with sound, MP3 music, games, television, e-mail, visual voice mail, and the Internet. (You can also talk on it!)

Samsung's new high-speed downlink transfers data from the Internet up to ten times faster than a normal cell phone. This makes video appear smoother.

NEXT GENERATION

A limited number of keys take up half a typical phone, and the screen the other half, so why not combine them? Models such as the Apple iPhone have one large touch-screen that uses liquid crystal technology. It flashes up an array of keys, buttons, icons (symbols), and menus, which you choose by touching lightly.

iPhone in dock

Cell phones constantly change the way we live. People can send important news, exchange pictures, fill time with games, and arrange to meet at short notice, almost anywhere.

TEXTING

When a text message, or short message service (SMS), is sent, it travels as codes of radio waves into the network via the nearest cell phone mast. The message is stored at a short message service center (SMSC), which regularly checks the phone of the person you're sending it to. When this is switched on and is in contact with the base transceiver station, the SMSC forwards the text message.

➤ *Cell phone towers usually have tall, slim, boxlike radio aerials and drum-shaped microwave dishes. To avoid spoiling a view, they can be disguised as trees!*

The transmitter is concealed within the "branches" of a fake pine tree.

➤ *Photos and videos taken on cell phones allow anyone to be a reporter, making it easy to capture an event as it happens and pass the images to the news channels.*

 ## CELLULAR NETWORK

The "cell" of the cell-phone system is the area around a base transceiver station (BTS). The BTS connects cell phones to the phone network by transmitting and receiving radio microwaves. When cell phone A calls cell phone B, cell phone A's closest BTS connects to the exchange. The exchange then finds the cell that cell phone B is in and routes the call to the BTS in that cell.

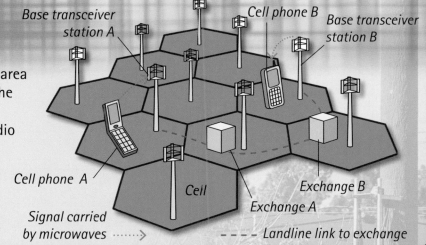

Base transceiver station A

Cell phone B

Base transceiver station B

Cell phone A

Cell

Exchange B

Exchange A

Signal carried by microwaves ·······>

– – – – Landline link to exchange

LAPTOP

You can use a laptop anywhere—on the train, in the yard, even in the bathroom! The modern laptop does almost anything a full-sized personal computer can do, plus it's portable, and with wireless links it has no trailing cables to trip over.

The development of smaller and more powerful silicon chips has made laptops possible. A laptop's overall size depends on the area of the liquid crystal display (LCD) screen.

Very thin thin film transistor (TFT) LCD screen

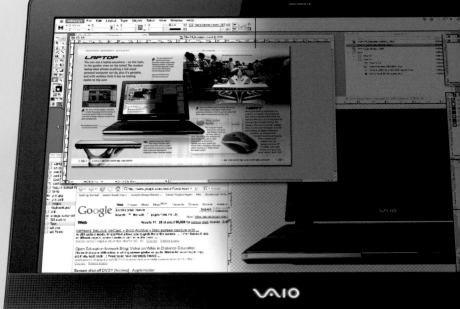

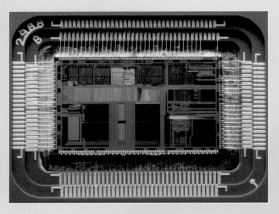

The "brain" of the laptop is the central processing unit (CPU). It is actually several chips in one casing, with rows of metal strips to connect it to other components.

Touch-sensitive trackpad

Laptops have style. Sony's Vaio range features ultramodern materials, such as carbon fiber, and has screen sizes ranging from a slim and lightweight notebook to a larger desktop version.

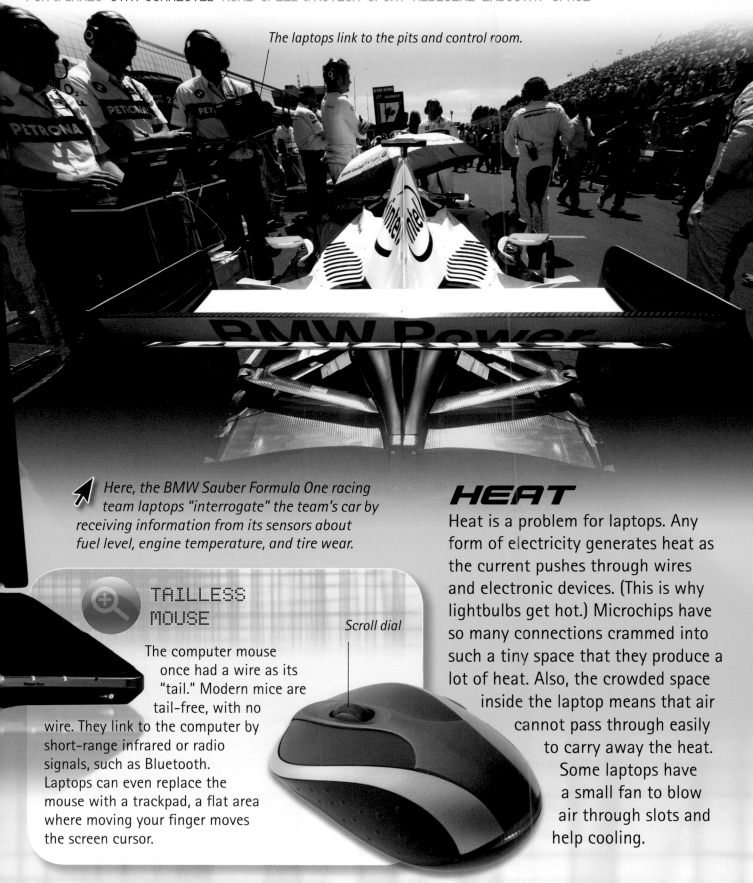

The laptops link to the pits and control room.

Here, the BMW Sauber Formula One racing team laptops "interrogate" the team's car by receiving information from its sensors about fuel level, engine temperature, and tire wear.

TAILLESS MOUSE

The computer mouse once had a wire as its "tail." Modern mice are tail-free, with no wire. They link to the computer by short-range infrared or radio signals, such as Bluetooth. Laptops can even replace the mouse with a trackpad, a flat area where moving your finger moves the screen cursor.

Scroll dial

HEAT

Heat is a problem for laptops. Any form of electricity generates heat as the current pushes through wires and electronic devices. (This is why lightbulbs get hot.) Microchips have so many connections crammed into such a tiny space that they produce a lot of heat. Also, the crowded space inside the laptop means that air cannot pass through easily to carry away the heat. Some laptops have a small fan to blow air through slots and help cooling.

WEBCAM

Link a digital camera with a microphone to the the Internet, and you have a webcam! It can send pictures and sounds to anyone in an instant. This means you can see and chat in real time, "live," to school friends down the road or someone half a world away.

Some webcams have automatic face tracking and focus. They recognize the features of a face, focus onto them, and keep the face in the middle of the view even if it moves to one side.

Autofocus camera lens

Carl Zeiss

Tessar 2.0/3.7

2MP Autofocus

FIRST WEBCAM

The first time a digital camera was linked to a computer network was in 1991, at the computer science department of Cambridge University, England. It helped scientists working in other rooms to see when their coffee was ready, using a specially designed program called "X-Coffee."

A coffeepot—the first blurred webcam image.

Webcams are placed above the monitor. Look into the camera as you speak, instead of staring down at your own screen, and you will appear more natural on the screen at the other end.

SPACECAMS

Since 1995 the Solar and Heliospheric Observatory (SOHO) satellite has watched the Sun from far out in space. Its cameras convert images of sunspots and solar flares into radio waves, which downlink to large satellite-tracking dishes around the world. The images are then uploaded to the Internet for anyone to view.

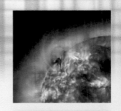

SOHO's cameras pick up not only visible light but also the shorter waves of ultraviolet light, here showing a solar eruption.

HOW IT WORKS

A webcam turns pictures and sounds into digital electronic pulses. Like a movie camera, it can "grab" a string of still images, many each second—it can then send them via a computer and the telecom system to the person you choose. Their computer converts the pulses back to images on the screen. Webcams are often used for security reasons, to watch banks, stores, and even school playgrounds.

Microphone to pick up sounds

Spoken words can be converted in the computer to written text that appears on screen.

In video messaging, several people link up by webcam and chat together in a video version of a telephone conference call. Seeing the other people reduces risks, such as mistaken or stolen identity.

Customer : Hello
Advisor: Good afternoon how can I help ...
Customer: I have a problem with ....

Customer Details
Gender: Female
Name: Mrs Smith
Operating System: Yes
Current Customer: Yes

BLACKBERRY

If you're hungry for information, you need a Blackberry. You can't eat it, but you can use it to check your planner, e-mail a message to a local pizza place, and phone your friends to come around for a feast.

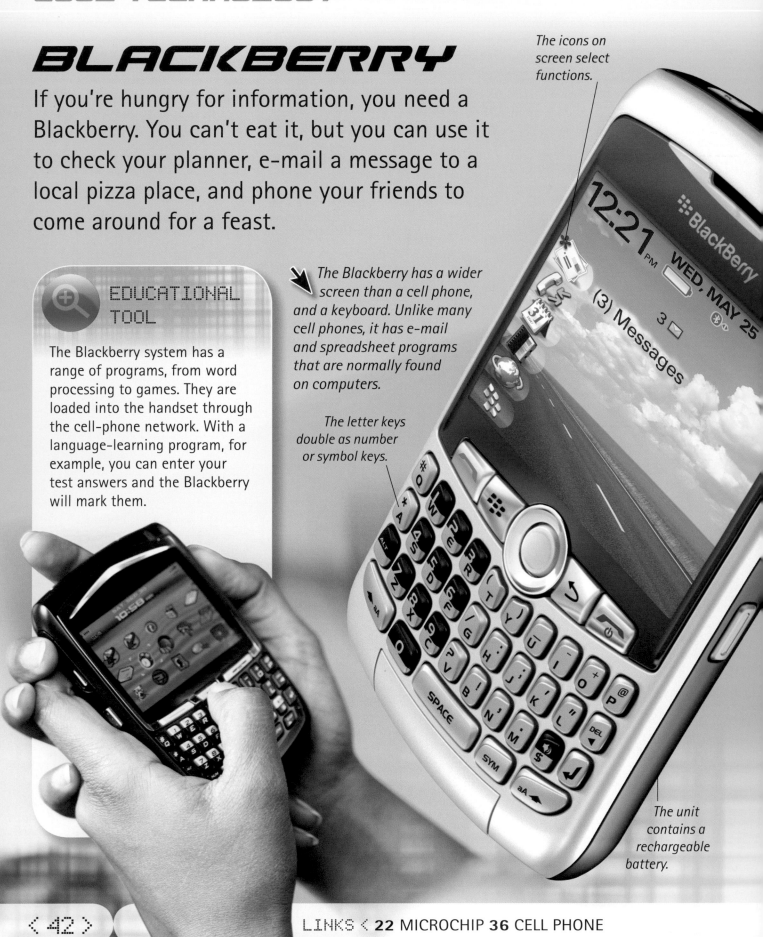

The icons on screen select functions.

EDUCATIONAL TOOL

The Blackberry system has a range of programs, from word processing to games. They are loaded into the handset through the cell-phone network. With a language-learning program, for example, you can enter your test answers and the Blackberry will mark them.

The Blackberry has a wider screen than a cell phone, and a keyboard. Unlike many cell phones, it has e-mail and spreadsheet programs that are normally found on computers.

The letter keys double as number or symbol keys.

The unit contains a rechargeable battery.

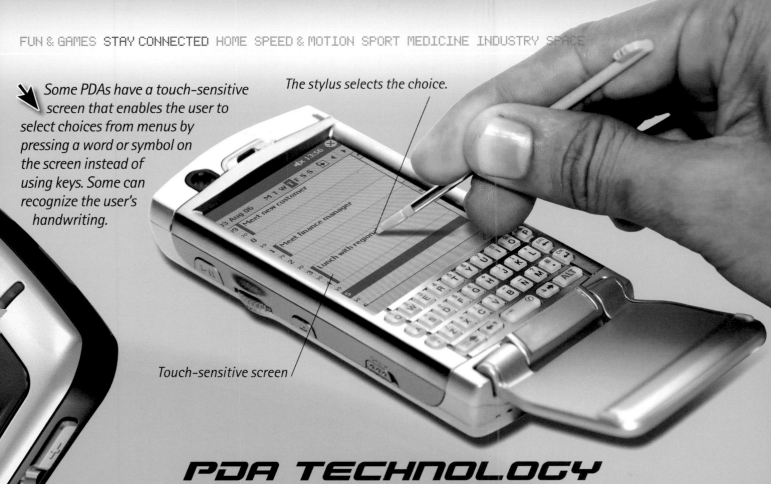

Some PDAs have a touch-sensitive screen that enables the user to select choices from menus by pressing a word or symbol on the screen instead of using keys. Some can recognize the user's handwriting.

The stylus selects the choice.

Touch-sensitive screen

Volume and brightness controls

PDA TECHNOLOGY

The Blackberry is one of a range of palm-sized gadgets called personal digital assistants (PDAs). These are handheld computers that work using digital wireless technology. PDA handsets link through the radio waves of the cell-phone network to a central control system, or server. Besides all the benefits of a cell phone, they can act as a diary and word processor and receive and send e-mails on the move.

RECOGNIZING WRITING

Writing on touch-sensitive screens requires a special set of pen strokes that the PDA can recognize. A sensor in the screen picks up the movements and converts them into digital text. The special strokes reduce errors, but most users find that keyboard input is faster.

The Graffiti recognition system

WIRELESS

Not so long ago, people were forever tripping over wires linking computers and other devices. Bluetooth connects devices, such as cell phones and computers, directly to each other. Wi-Fi connects devices to networks, such as the Internet.

BLUETOOTH

The Bluetooth system makes wireless connections between computers and their equipment or cell phones and headsets, over distances of several feet. The most recent Bluetooth version (2.1) has better security and "pairing," when devices recognize each other. It also allows longer battery life when devices wait on standby, in low-power mode.

Bluetooth headsets enable hands-free talking to a local source station, such as a cordless phone base many feet away.

Hands-free headsets make talking while driving or working machinery much safer.

WI-FI ALLIANCE

This laptop user is connecting to the Internet from a public place via Wi-Fi. The power, speed, and other features of Wi-Fi equipment are checked and regulated by a group of companies known as the Wi-Fi Alliance. They make sure that gadgets labeled "Wi-Fi" connect easily and work together properly.

< 44 >
ESSENTIAL FOR > laptop · Blackberry · Wii · cell-phone headset

HOW WI-FI HOTSPOTS WORK

Signs at airports, ports, railroad stations, shopping malls, offices, and city centers say "Wi-Fi Hotspot." This wireless local-area network (LAN) uses radio signals to link wireless-enabled gadgets to the Internet. A wireless device, such as a laptop or PDA, scans the radio spectrum (range) and locks onto the signals from a nearby aerial, or antenna. You can then check your e-mails or surf the Web.

3 The aerials are connected to the hotspot router. This is a faster version of the router in a home or office. It is linked into the main Internet.

4 The system recognizes the user's password and encrypts messages, changing them into code so others at the hotspot cannot see them.

2 The signals come from several aerials around the hotspot, which usually have a limited range, perhaps a few tens of yards.

1 A wireless-enabled laptop, Internet phone, or PDA can scan for suitable radio links in an area and begin the connection.

ROUTERS

A wireless router is a radio transceiver (transmitter-receiver) linked to the Internet and other communications networks. It sends and receives information and keeps track of the different devices connected to it so there are no mix-ups.

SMART CARD

Smart cards contain a microchip that stores data, such as your name and address or the balance in your bank account. They have many uses, from payment to security checks. Smart cards in cell phones are called SIM cards.

A bank smart card has a wafer-thin microchip inside. The chip is beneath a gold contact pad— eight areas covered with thin gold metal that connect to the card reader.

Gold contact pad

Microchip

SMART BANKING

An automatic teller machine (ATM) is a computer version of the cashier inside the bank. It's not just a teller substitute for taking out money. By using a bank smart card, you can also put money into an account, pay bills, move money between accounts, and top up your cell phone.

ATMs can be accessed 24 hours a day.

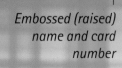

BANK of CITYTOW
Credit Card

expires

valid from

The microchip is glued onto a plastic support.

Embossed (raised) name and card number

SIM CARDS

A SIM card contains a subscriber identity module—a microchip that holds data special to an individual. SIM cards in cell phones store data, such as the phone's number, phonebook contacts, text messages, and phone settings. Switching a SIM card from one phone to another carries all this information with it. Most SIM cards work using Global System for Mobile communications (GSM) technology. This is a standard way of turning information into digital codes used by cell-phone networks around the world.

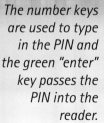

Security hologram

 A SIM card slots into a metal sleeve in a cell phone. Subscriber information on the card identifies the owner to the network.

A cell phone SIM is about 1 inch (25 mm) tall, ½ inch (15 mm) wide, and 0.76 mm—a lot less than ¼ inch—thick.

The number keys are used to type in the PIN and the green "enter" key passes the PIN into the reader.

CHIP AND PIN

Information is put into and taken from smart bank cards by a chip and PIN reader. To make sure whoever uses the card is its real owner, they must key in their own unique personal identity number (PIN). This usually has four digits (numbers). People should never write down their PIN and carry it with the card—that makes crime too easy!

SPEECH RECOGNITION

We hear people speak, and understand what they mean, almost without thinking. Speech recognition technology allows computers to do the same. It detects the sounds of a voice, separates out the words, and works out what is meant.

Voice sounds are changed into electrical signals and shown on-screen as a sonogram or "voiceprint." Each person's voice looks different.

SPEAK-WRITE SOFTWARE

Some people cannot use the usual keyboard to enter words into a computer, perhaps because they are injured or disabled. Speak-write software automatically converts their spoken words into written ones. Speech commands can also be used to control machines and gadgets.

A disabled person training to use speak-write software

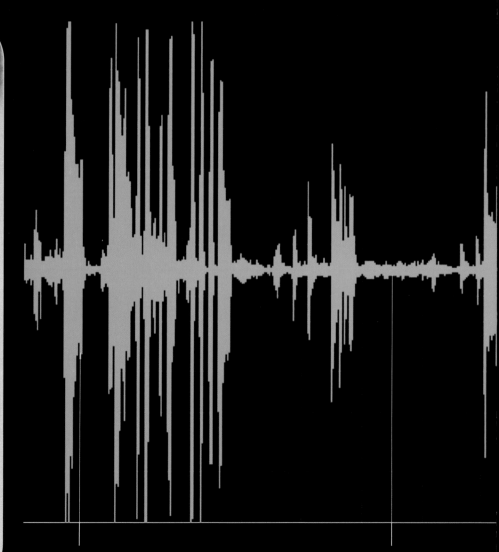

The height of the line shows the loudness of the sound.

The short lines only show background noise.

SPEECH-CONTROLLED MILITARY ROBOTS

The PackBot Scout is a voice-controlled surveillance robot used to "sniff" for explosives in dangerous areas. Its software recognizes commands, such as "stop" and "go," and sends back live sound and video. This reduces the risk of soldiers setting off explosives that have been booby trapped. The robot is also used to search for signs of life in disaster zones.

Crawler treads for rough ground

SEP 15 2001
11:23:47 PM

A PackBot being used in a search and rescue mission.

PROBLEMS WITH SPEECH

Speech recognition software needs "training" to recognize its user's voice and ways of saying words. The user reads out a series of phrases so the computer gets used to the accent, volume, and speed of the speech. Even so, speech sounds can change if we are hurried, shouting, or whispering. Voice recognition means identifying an individual person's vocal sounds as a "voiceprint," like identifying fingerprints.

This walking Japanese toy robot, called Nuvo, was launched in 2004. It can recognize more than 1,000 voice commands, such as "dance," "bow," and "get up," and it can even be controlled remotely from a cell phone.

Many tall lines together indicate a "stop" or "plosive" sound.

DIGITAL RADIO

Sending sound through radio waves was achieved over 100 years ago. For a long time radio sounded crackly, but the invention of transistors, followed by digital audio broadcasting (DAB), has transformed the sound of the radio.

A DAB radio set can be complete in one casing, or it may have separate units—the receiver, plus two speakers placed apart for better stereo sound.

The receiver detects the radio waves.

DAB WAVES

Analogue radio transmits sound with varying radio waves. In amplitude modulation (AM), the strength or height of the radio wave varies; in frequency modulation (FM), the number of waves per second varies. Digital radio is different. First, sound is encoded as a pattern of 0s and 1s, then DAB uses thousands of on-off pulses per second to transmit the data.

Socket for headphones

The scan button tracks through radio stations.

A DJ's DAB control console feeds digital signals directly into a computer.

The function control switches between digital radio (DAB), older analogue radio (FM/AM), and CD (compact disc).

DAB UPGRADE

Although DAB radios have been available only since 1999, the DAB technology was developed in the 1980s. From 2008, an improved technology known as DAB+ will be introduced internationally. DAB+ is almost three times more efficient, providing higher audio quality, even better reception, and more stations.

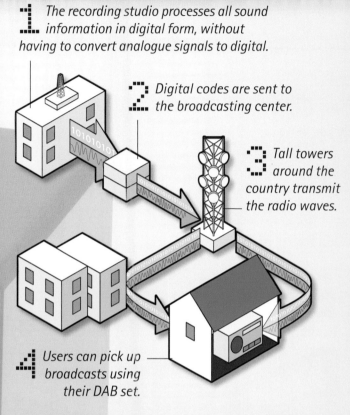

STUDIO > RADIO

1 The recording studio processes all sound information in digital form, without having to convert analogue signals to digital.

2 Digital codes are sent to the broadcasting center.

3 Tall towers around the country transmit the radio waves.

4 Users can pick up broadcasts using their DAB set.

All radio waves pick up interference as they travel through the air. When DAB broadcasts are decoded by a DAB radio, the interference diminishes. This is one of the advantages of digital over analogue. Digital radio is also rebroadcast by cable and satellite TV companies, so listeners can tune in with their televisions. Computer users can also listen to digital radio over the Internet.

DAB information includes not only sounds, but the time and date, the radio station playing, its type of music, the latest news, and more!

Station information

12:01   08/20/2008
CAPITAL FM
ROCK/POP

NOW PLAYING... LINKIN PARK

MEMORY POWER

We all need memory. How else could we store data, recall it, learn, and progress? Computers and electronic gadgets are the same. It's not only the amount of memory that is important, but how fast these gadgets can find information, known as retrieval time.

Flash drives are memory microchips protected in a casing. They are used for all kinds of data, including pictures and video.

STORING MEMORY

Information in a microchip can take up less than one-millionth of the space of the same information on paper. The whole set of instructions to build the human body, the human genome (decoded DNA), fills these library shelves as pages in files—but the same information can be stored in just one thumb-size flash drive.

Computer memory is unlikely ever to replace paper entirely; people will always want a "hard copy."

USB (universal serial bus) connection plugs into computer.

The strong plastic casing protects the chip from damage.

256 MB

Memory cards use flash memory just like flash drives, but they are thinner and so will fit into small devices, such as digital cameras and video cameras.

PRACTICAL MEMORY

The pocket-size Swiss Army Knife is famous for holding many useful items, from blades to corkscrew, in one handy casing. A recent addition is the memory stick, which must be as tough as the rest of the knife, waterproof, and shockproof. It can hold information, such as the owner's medical details, in case of an emergency.

The 2-GB flash drive folds away.

Supercomputers have memories and processors organized into closet-size casings. This 2004 NASA supercomputer is good at "number crunching." It can do trillions of calculations per second and helps engineers work out how spacecraft will perform.

SUPERCOMPUTERS

A typical home computer has one processor, 2 gigabytes (GB) of working memory (RAM) and a hard disk that can store 250 GB. The NASA supercomputer (see below) has 10,240 processors, 20 terabytes (20,000 GB) of RAM, 440 terabytes of storage, and 10 petabytes (10 million GB) of archive storage—but it was only the 13th most powerful computer in the world as of June 2007.

Slots allow cool air to pass over hot microchips and circuits.

INTERNET

The Internet is a network of networks. It allows computers, cameras, and other devices around the world to be linked. It uses radio waves and laser flashes along optical fibers, and electrical signals along wires. They "talk" in the digital code of 1s and 0s.

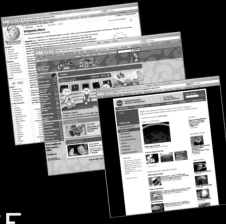

Web sites carry text, video, images, sound, and anything that can be sent via digital code by servers (above).

MULTI-USE

The Internet has made it much easier to find, create, and share information. Information on different Web sites can also be combined, showing traffic reports from one source on maps from another, for example. It can access television and radio from anywhere, and it also carries communication between people by e-mail or Voice-over-Internet protocol (VOIP).

| E-mail | File sharing | Surfing | Messaging | VOIP |

These icons show some of the Internet's uses. VOIP is for making a phone call via the Internet.

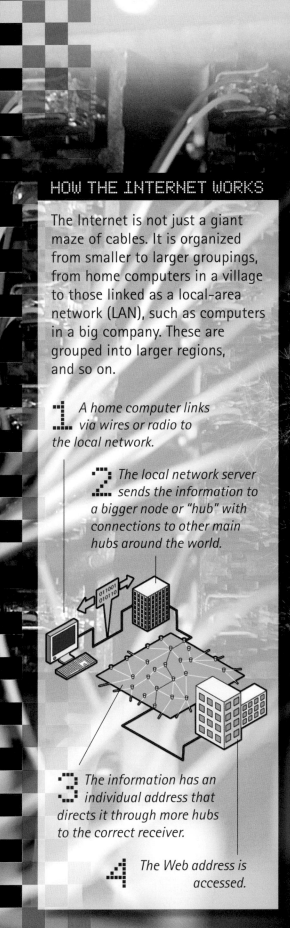

HOW THE INTERNET WORKS

The Internet is not just a giant maze of cables. It is organized from smaller to larger groupings, from home computers in a village to those linked as a local-area network (LAN), such as computers in a big company. These are grouped into larger regions, and so on.

1 *A home computer links via wires or radio to the local network.*

2 *The local network server sends the information to a bigger node or "hub" with connections to other main hubs around the world.*

3 *The information has an individual address that directs it through more hubs to the correct receiver.*

4 *The Web address is accessed.*

< 54 >

ESSENTIAL FOR > GPS · laptop · Blackberry · webcam

WORLDWIDE WEB

This diagram illustrates the density of Internet routes in one region of a country. Bright areas are local servers that link into the larger Web. It is easy to see how the Web provides such freedom—it is almost impossible to stop people talking or sharing information!

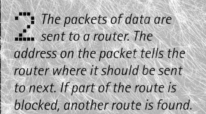

2 *The packets of data are sent to a router. The address on the packet tells the router where it should be sent to next. If part of the route is blocked, another route is found.*

3 *Sometimes packets from the same set take different routes. Eventually, the routers pass all the packets along to their destination, where their data can be reassembled.*

1 *Most of the Internet uses "packet switching." Data, such as text on a Web page, is broken into small packets of data, each with its destination address and information on how to fit it back together.*

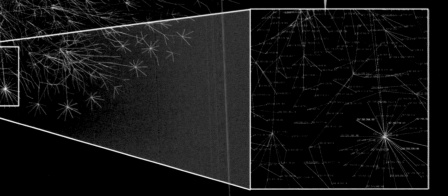

SATPHONE

Reporting from a war zone and all communications networks have been knocked out? Studying penguins at the South Pole? That's no problem if you have a satellite phone, because instead of using cell-phone towers, a satphone's signals are carried by satellites orbiting the Earth.

This small waterproof case houses a satellite transmitter-receiver, an adjustable camera aimed at the reporter, a monitor screen, and a rechargeable battery for electricity.

Monitor screen

Phone handset

INSTANT NEWS

Satphones are mainly used by news reporters. In disaster zones or very remote places, there is often no electricity or cell-phone network. The satphone

has a battery for power, and does not need cell-phone masts. Ships also carry satphones connected to microwave antennae (aerials) on masts, which automatically track satellites.

On this satphone, the case opens out to form a satellite receiver.

VIDEO SATPHONE

A video satphone is a portable video-with-sound camera connected to a briefcase-size transmitter that sends radio signals high into space. The signals are received by one or more satellites in an orbiting pattern. The satellite strengthens the signals and beams them down to a huge dish at a satellite tracking station. This passes them to the television company for broadcast.

The camera is turned to face the reporter.

The extra-large antenna links by radio waves to the nearest Iridium satellite.

IRIDIUM PHONE

The Iridium system has 66 orbiting satellites to allow worldwide communication from handheld satellite phones. The system is unique in that it covers the whole Earth. The satellites orbit about 485 miles (780 km) up and send and receive radio signals from the Earth, passing the information among themselves as needed.

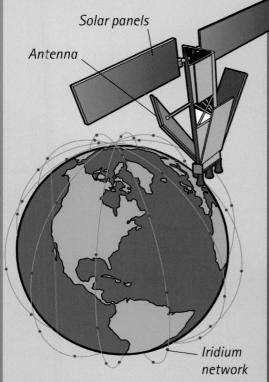

Solar panels

Antenna

Iridium network

The whole Iridium setup is known as a satellite constellation. Each satellite can carry more than 1,000 phone calls.

Iridium cell phones carry voice calls, text messages, and some Internet information anywhere in the world—even in the middle of the oceans or on the polar ice caps.

COMMUNICATIONS SATELLITE

Communications satellites receive radio or microwave signals from a satellite station on an uplink, and send them on a downlink to another station far away, or broadcast them to a wide area.

Solar panels generate electricity from sunlight.

🔍 DISH RECEIVERS

Smaller satellite dishes are mounted on many tall buildings, towers, and other high places where there is less interference for their radio waves. Some dishes are only receivers—for example, for satellite television. Others both transmit (send) and receive—for example, for phone calls and for exchanging computer data.

Owners of tall buildings rent out their roof space for satellite dish users.

Dishes receive and transmit radio waves.

A communications satellite has several transponder (transmitter-responder) channels. Each can carry several TV channels or hundreds of phone calls. Satellites are owned by organizations such as Intelsat.

The main body of the satellite is called its bus.

⇒ *Satellites are sent into space by launch vehicles, such as rockets or space shuttles. Sometimes a satellite breaks down, drifts from orbit, or needs updating. Getting an astronaut to fix it and install new equipment may be cheaper than launching a new satellite.*

Space shuttle robot arm

Astronaut in space suit

TRACKING

Some satellites pass overhead every few hours. Satellite dishes on the Earth can be tilted by electric motors to keep tracking (pointing at) them. Other satellites do not seem to move at all. They are in geostationary orbit (GEO) about 22,250 miles (35,800 km) above the equator. Here, the satellite goes around the Earth at the same speed as the Earth spins, once in 24 hours, so the satellite seems to hover in the same place, and dishes can be fixed to point at it.

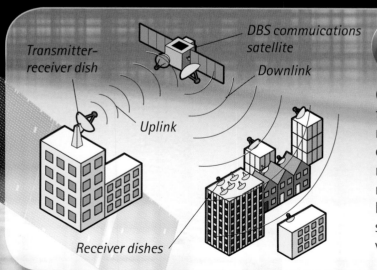

Transmitter-receiver dish

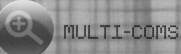
DBS commuications satellite

Uplink

Downlink

Receiver dishes

MULTI-COMS

Communications satellites carry any information that can be changed into codes of radio signals or microwaves. This includes voice calls, videophone calls, photographs and pictures, television and radio programs, movies, and computer files. What many people call satellite television is received by home dishes straight from a direct broadcast satellite (DBS). The DBS beams its waves over a very large area, known as a footprint.

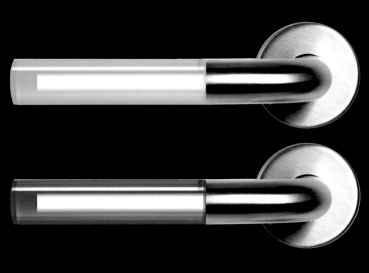

BRIGHTHANDLE 72-73

INTELLIGENT REFRIGERATOR 70-71

MICRO APARTMENT 68-69

CYCLONIC VACUUM CLEANER 76-77

HOME

Home is where people have always relaxed, cooked, bathed, and slept. But the hi-tech homes of today would be unrecognizable to someone from just 50 years ago. Intelligent home gadgets make chores quicker and easier, robot toys keep us entertained, and the buildings themselves are ever better at saving energy and conserving our natural resources.

ECO HOME

As we become more aware of the damage humans are doing to the environment, more and more of us want to live in "eco" homes. These are built from sustainable materials, waste less energy, and make the most of natural resources, such as sunlight, wind, and rain.

Modern eco homes are made of "low-impact" materials, such as wood, which need little energy to manufacture or prepare.

Solar panels convert sunlight to electricity.

The wind turbine generates electricity.

Sun-facing windows trap and store heat like a greenhouse.

INSULATION

°C
9
8
7
6
5
4
3

Seen in infrared, an insulated home (above right) loses less heat.

Heating bills can be one-fourth of a home's running costs. Insulation slows the passage of heat to the outside, reducing energy loss and, therefore, cost. Walls and roofs are insulated with sheets of fiberglass or expanded-foam plastics. These trap warm air, preventing it from leaking out. Likewise, double-glazed windows sandwich a layer of air between two panes and trap heat.

ECO COMMUNITY

Houses can sometimes work together to save resources and energy. Shared pipes carry hot water for washing and heating, and waste water is partly recycled. Built from natural or recycled materials, eco houses have large windows facing the sun to make the best use of heat and light, and small windows on the non-sunny sides. The outer walls are well insulated.

This eco-housing community is in Beddington, near London.

Air outlets cool the house in hot weather, without the need for air-conditioning.

Wood cladding provides good weatherproofing and insulation.

ZERO CARBON

Coal, oil, and gas are all made from carbon. As they burn in heating systems, cars, and power stations, the carbon combines with oxygen in the air to form carbon dioxide—a greenhouse gas. This traps heat in the Earth's atmosphere, causing global warming. Eco homes are designed to use energy sources that don't generate greenhouse gases, such as solar power, wind turbines, and hydroelectricity (electricity generated from moving water).

Organic roof covering provides natural waterproofing and insulation.

Purifying water so that it is safe to drink requires energy and chemicals. But many tasks, such as cleaning cars or watering plants, don't need pure water, so it makes sense to collect free rainwater from the roof and use this instead.

< 63 >

SOLAR CELL

A solar cell, also called a photovoltaic cell, is a device that converts light energy into electrical energy. Solar power reduces the need for fossil fuels, which contribute to global warming, but can be unreliable in countries where there is little sunshine.

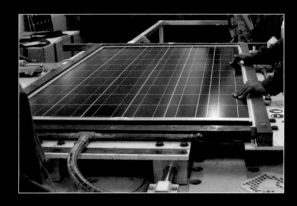

Solar cells are made in clean conditions, using very pure materials. This makes them costly to produce.

SOLAR PANELS

A single solar cell can produce enough energy to power a pocket calculator. Solar cells can be joined together to form larger solar panels, which can provide enough energy to power a house. The energy produced by solar panels is collected in rechargeable batteries—these are charged up during the day, when the Sun shines, to provide energy for use at night.

Solar panels are colored blue to enable them to absorb as much sunlight as possible.

SOLAR WALLS

These solar panels form the facade of a modern office building and face south to catch the sun for most of the day. The electricity is stored in batteries and used to power low-voltage lights and computers.

< 64 >
ESSENTIAL FOR > pocket calculators · eco homes

HOW SOLAR CELLS WORK

All matter is made from tiny particles called atoms, which contain even tinier particles, including electrons. Electricity is the movement of electrons between atoms. A solar cell contains two layers of a substance called silicon. When sunlight falls on the cell, the electrons are pushed from one layer to the other by the light energy. Because silicon's surface naturally reflects light, an antireflective coating also has to be added to let the light in.

1 Sunlight shines on two layers of silicon. The upper one contains tiny amounts of one chemical (such as phosphorous) to make it negative; the lower layer contains another chemical (such as boron) to make it positive.

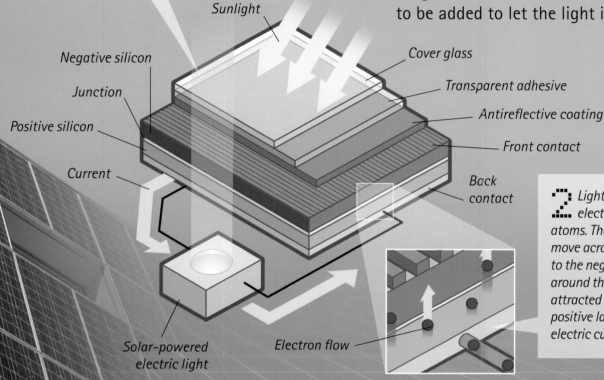

Sunlight

Negative silicon

Junction

Positive silicon

Current

Cover glass

Transparent adhesive

Antireflective coating

Front contact

Back contact

Solar-powered electric light

Electron flow

2 Light energy knocks electrons off their atoms. These free electrons move across the junction to the negative layer, go around the circuit, and are attracted back to the positive layer. This is an electric current.

SIMPLER PRODUCTION = CHEAPER CELLS

At the moment, the high cost of producing solar cells makes solar power an expensive option, but a new type of cell could change that. The Nanosolar SolarPly can be printed directly onto flexible sheets, which means that rolls of lightweight solar panels could be produced more cheaply than traditional solar cells.

Solar cells cover every roof in this modern American eco-housing community.

AMAZING FACT > Concave mirrors were used in the late 15th century to heat water.

< 65 >

REVOLVING APARTMENT

How would you like a room with a view that changes without you ever having to leave your bed? This luxury is enjoyed by residents of the Suite Vollard in Curitiba, Brazil. Here, each separate apartment can revolve at the touch of a button.

The control display shows a map of each apartment, which way it's facing, and how fast it's turning in either direction. It can be programmed by the touch screen or by voice command.

The turning time for one rotation can be adjusted from 15 minutes to one hour.

The outer, ringlike part of the apartment can rotate in a full circle, clockwise or counterclockwise, according to the owner's instructions.

The core of the tower stays still.

LIFE IN A SPIN

Inside an apartment

Each apartment's outer ring revolves under the complete control of the owner. It is driven by large electric motors that turn nylon wheels pressing on metal rails under the floor, so the movement is quiet and smooth. The immobile inner area of each apartment contains the kitchen and bathroom, so the pipes do not twist around. Lights and air-conditioning are also programmable.

MICRO LIVING

When people only need to live somewhere for a short time, why waste space and resources on a large house? A micro home is a living, cooking, and sleeping space all provided in one roomy box.

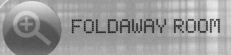

FOLDAWAY ROOM

The table folds to make room for beds.

The space inside the micro home changes depending on which parts you fold out. There is a sliding table, a fully equipped kitchen area, a shower cubicle and toilet, and two double beds. All this fits in a square box 8¾ feet (2.7 m) long, wide, and tall.

The micro home's wooden frame and aluminum covering make it very light and easy for a crane to lift. Solar panels on the roof provide plenty of electricity.

The connecting pole is for stacking micro homes.

Tough aluminum panels are insulated to keep in the warmth.

Micro homes can be stacked on strong stilts, with connecting stairs.

LINKS ‹ 62 ECO HOME 64 SOLAR CELL

MICRO HOMES

Soaring house prices in big cities make it hard for people to find affordable homes, so a small living space—a micro apartment—that costs less to buy or rent makes good economic sense. A micro apartment also costs less to maintain, heat, and clean than a large apartment—and it uses less energy. Modular housing, where micro apartments are stacked together on site, helps to cut buying and running costs.

WINDOW ON LIFE

This micro home displayed in a department store.

To test micro-apartment life, volunteers are monitored by TV cameras. A computer speeds up people's movements. The observers study how the residents move about, which areas they use most, how they organize tasks, such as cooking a meal, and which parts become too crowded, to help improve the design.

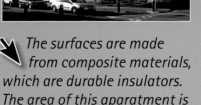

Micro apartments in a modular housing unit are stacked by crane and connected to utilities, such as electricity, water, and drainage.

The surfaces are made from composite materials, which are durable insulators. The area of this aparatment is only 345 square feet (32 sq m).

The utility pod has a range of storage compartments.

The main area functions as a kitchen, living room, and home office.

The large, double-glazed "window wall" lets in plenty of natural light.

The sliding wall panels lead into the double bedroom.

INTELLIGENT KITCHEN

Kitchens can use over half of a home's energy. Heat for cooking, electricity for refrigerators and other gadgets, and hot and cold water are all expensive. The smart kitchen uses low-energy appliances that save electricity and speed up cooking.

The thinking refrigerator has a touch screen for TV and the Internet. When items run out, you can re-order them online.

The refrigerator's computer can suggest recipes and warn of power outages or out-of-date food.

FOLDAWAY KITCHEN

The lights switch on as the doors open.

This kitchen can be installed in the corner of a living room.

In most small homes, the kitchen is only used for a short time to prepare meals. A foldaway kitchen is a single ready-to-use unit. The stovetop and oven share heat, water can be partly recycled, the microwave saves cooking energy and the extractor fan draws away smells. When the doors are closed, there's instant extra living space.

The Futuristic Kitchen by Gorenje can be put into a home, or into the corner of a larger hall, or sited in a public place for a time—then taken away.

ALL IN ONE

Older kitchens with separate appliances, such as oven, refrigerator, and microwave, take time to keep clean—often using strong cleaning chemicals that can harm the environment. The smooth, wipe-clean surfaces of Gorenje's Futuristic Kitchen reduce both cleaning time and chemicals. The whole kitchen is a single round-cornered unit made from composite materials, similar to those used in spacecraft, and comes complete with appliances. Delivered by truck, it can be used outside or installed into a room.

The oven and microwave are at eye level to reduce stooping.

gorenje   ora-ïto

There is plenty of storage behind see-through doors.

The ceramic stovetop has a wipe-clean glass cover.

Overhead lamp

The flexi-faucet delivers hot and cold water.

With clever design, a kitchen can be reduced to a "workbench" area with a stovetop, double sink, and preparation areas. It can even fold up against a wall.

The main work-surface area has an antiscratch surface.

BATHROOM

Lavatories can be a nuisance to clean—and there's always the risk of the toilet paper running out. A smart toilet turns the bathroom experience into a pleasure, and a smart shower keeps you clean and warm, while saving water.

The Neorest toilet's motion sensor will automatically lift the lid and turn on music as you approach, then it will lower the lid, flush the toilet, and freshen the air as you leave.

A powerful "cyclone" flush action cleans the whole pan.

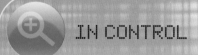

IN CONTROL

Multifunction buttons control the toilet.

Hi-tech toilets respond at the touch of a button. Instead of toilet paper, there's a fine spray with adjustable temperature and pressure to clean yourself hygienically. This is followed by warm air for drying. The seat temperature can be controlled for comfort, and an air freshener is built in. There's even a radio and MP3 sound system to enjoy while you sit.

MODERN SHOWER

A shower uses only about one-third of the hot water needed to fill a bathtub, and it gets you cleaner, too. Super showers have sensors that keep the water at a temperature that can be programmed for each user. The jet pattern uses less water yet gives an all-over spray.

➡ *When the super shower cubicle is empty, infrared sensors turn the water off automatically, unless the manual override button is pressed.*

GLOW HANDLES

On the outside of a lavatory or bathroom, the clear acrylic end of the Brighthandle glows red when the door is locked by a user inside. When the door unlocks, a green light illuminates the handle. This saves a person having to jiggle the handle to see if the door is locked.

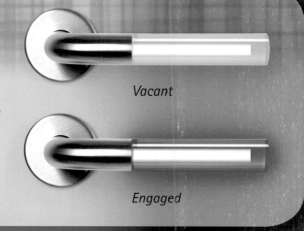

Vacant

Engaged

The display can be set to pounds or kilograms.

↖ *Digital scales display your weight as numbers on a small screen. The memory stores the previous weights for all users, each of whom has an individual code.*

AUTOMATED HOME

Even an empty home can devour energy. There are electrical appliances on standby, and timer-controlled heating still comes on as usual. The auto home solves these problems with its sensors and programs, all conveniently under a central control.

HOW X10 WORKS

X10 is a system used to automate the home. It uses household electricity to carry messages between appliances. A remote control sends radio messages to a transceiver (transmitter-receiver), which passes them into an electric circuit. The messages are sent in the form of brief extra pulses of electricity on top of the normal main current. Messages are detected by receivers in equipment, such as heaters or lights, to turn them on or off.

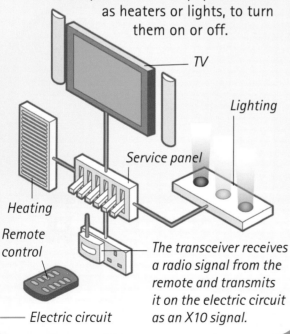

TV

Lighting

Service panel

Heating

Remote control

The transceiver receives a radio signal from the remote and transmits it on the electric circuit as an X10 signal.

— Electric circuit

1 Motion sensors, security light, and intercom.
2 Smart kitchen appliances linked to the Internet.
3 Digital wall screen changes picture according to mood.
4 Home entertainment system can access on-demand TV and central DVD library.
5 Surround sound in every room.
6 Satellite dish receives digital HDTV and DAB radio.
7 Outside speakers under voice command.
8 Automatic watering for plants.
9 Outdoor lighting controlled by motion sensor.
10 Wi-Fi access to Internet and central control.
11 TVs in each room linked to central system.
12 Home office with controls for all systems.
13 Intelligent bathroom with programmable water-saving toilet and shower and underfloor heating.
14 Thermostat controls temperature for entire house.

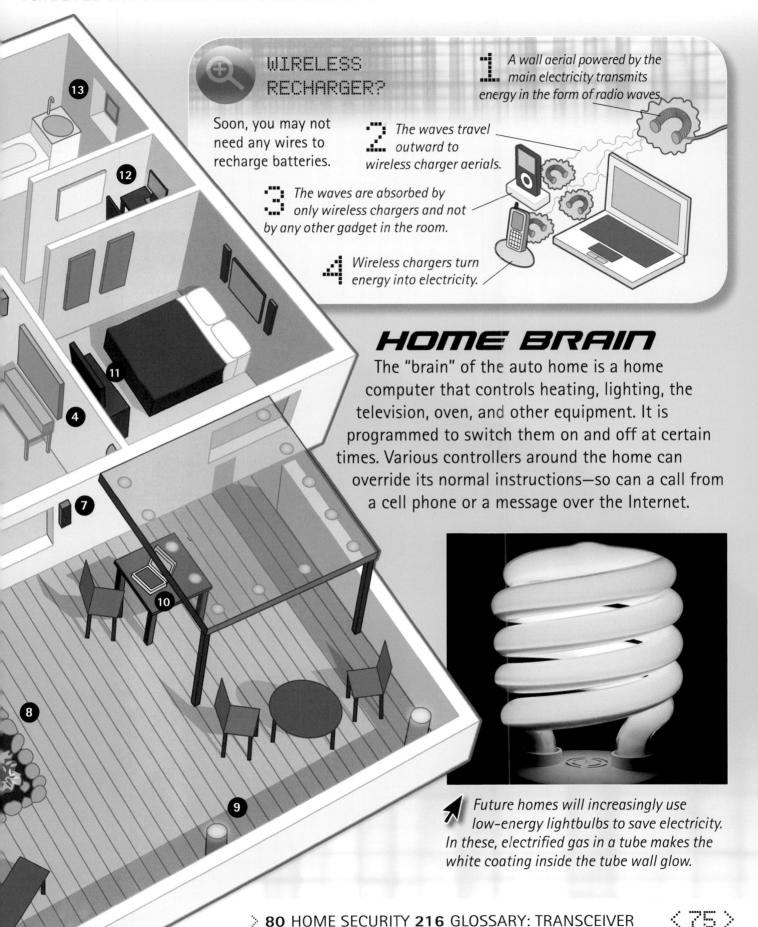

WIRELESS RECHARGER?

Soon, you may not need any wires to recharge batteries.

1 A wall aerial powered by the main electricity transmits energy in the form of radio waves.

2 The waves travel outward to wireless charger aerials.

3 The waves are absorbed by only wireless chargers and not by any other gadget in the room.

4 Wireless chargers turn energy into electricity.

HOME BRAIN

The "brain" of the auto home is a home computer that controls heating, lighting, the television, oven, and other equipment. It is programmed to switch them on and off at certain times. Various controllers around the home can override its normal instructions—so can a call from a cell phone or a message over the Internet.

Future homes will increasingly use low-energy lightbulbs to save electricity. In these, electrified gas in a tube makes the white coating inside the tube wall glow.

VACUUM

A vacuum cleaner's powerful fan sucks in air, creating a partial vacuum that more air rushes to fill. The fast-moving airflow sucks dirt particles into a bag or cylinder. Cylinders are much more efficient.

The Dyson cleaner's whirling action is modeled on the action of cyclone winds. These fast-moving, spinning columns of air suck up objects as they move along.

The clear main drum clips off for easy emptying.

The ball wheel allows precise steering into corners.

The cleaning brush can be adjusted for hard floors or carpets.

CYCLONIC ACTION

The air spins back up the middle and away.

The rotating airflow in the outer drum catches the larger particles.

1 Sucked-in air enters the outer drum at an angle, spinning around and down. **2** Larger dirt particles are flung against the wall and fall into the outer collector. **3** As the air enters the upside-down cones, it spins around at increasing speed and smaller bits of dust are collected at the cone tips.

Wheels keep the suction head close to the ground.

< 76 > LINKS < 48 VOICE RECOGNITION

PET SOUNDS

Gadgets can help our pets in many ways. A dog translator compares a dog's bark with a databank of "bark-prints" to suggest what the dog is trying to say. It's helpful and fun, but should not be taken too seriously!

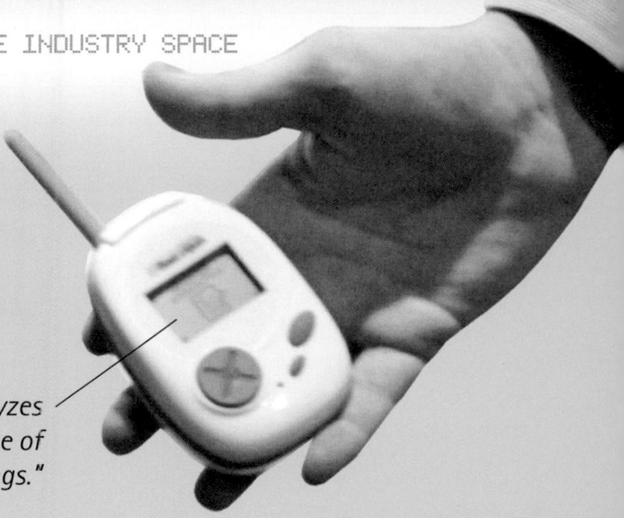

The receiver analyzes and displays one of six bark "meanings."

Happy
Needy
Sad
On guard
Frustrated
Assertive

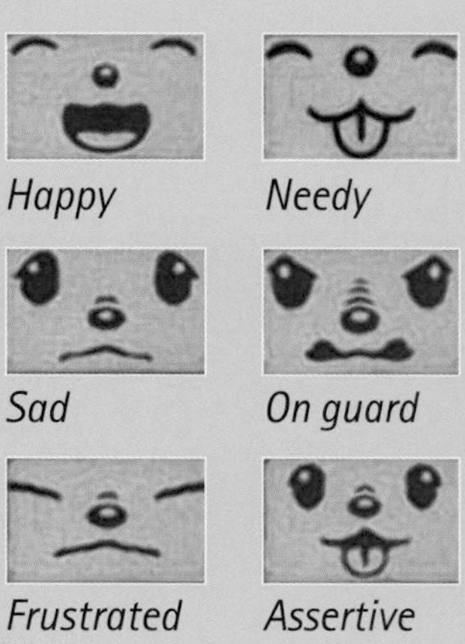

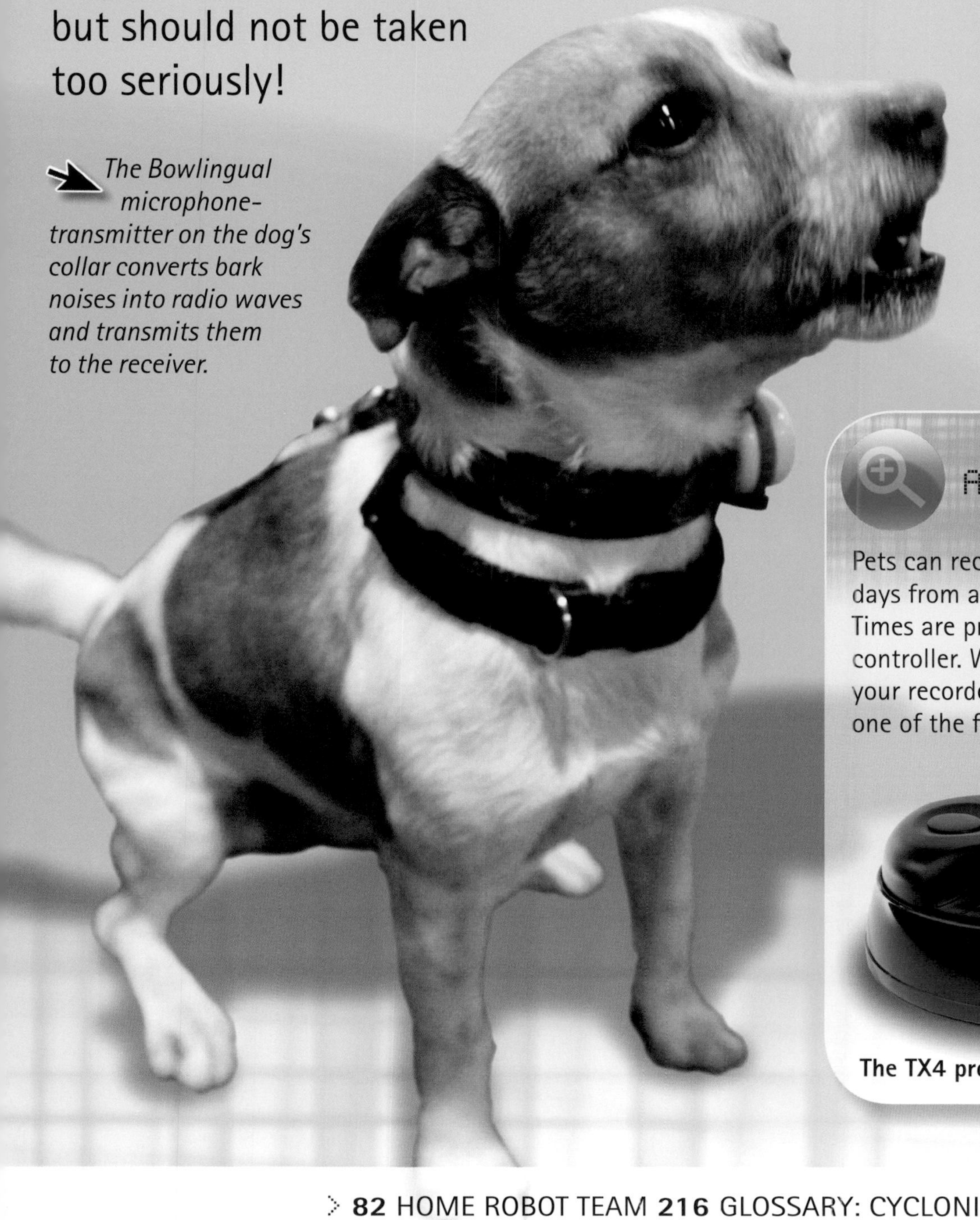

The Bowlingual microphone-transmitter on the dog's collar converts bark noises into radio waves and transmits them to the receiver.

AUTO PET FEEDER

Pets can receive meals for a few days from a robotic dispenser. Times are programmed into a controller. When mealtime arrives, your recorded voice calls out, and one of the four flaps opens.

The TX4 provides up to four meals.

> **82** HOME ROBOT TEAM **216** GLOSSARY: CYCLONIC MOTION

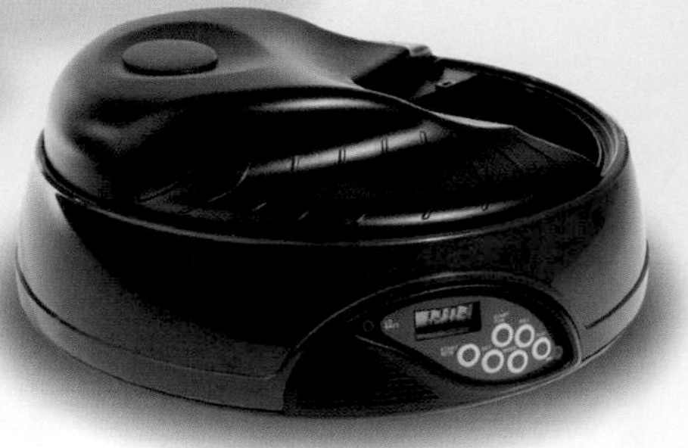

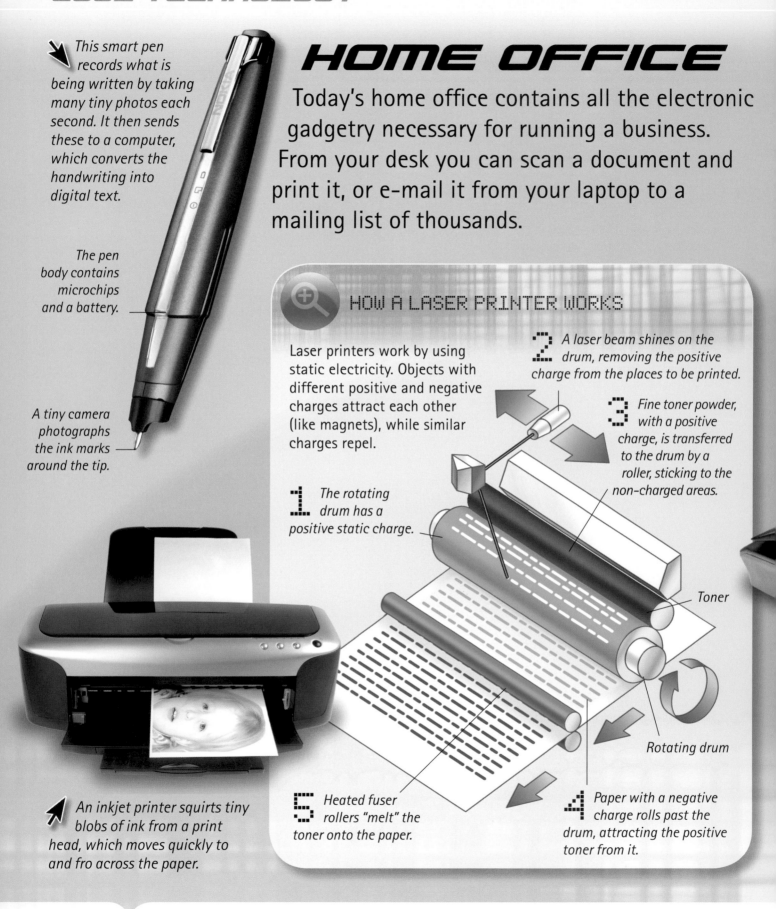

This smart pen records what is being written by taking many tiny photos each second. It then sends these to a computer, which converts the handwriting into digital text.

The pen body contains microchips and a battery.

A tiny camera photographs the ink marks around the tip.

HOME OFFICE

Today's home office contains all the electronic gadgetry necessary for running a business. From your desk you can scan a document and print it, or e-mail it from your laptop to a mailing list of thousands.

HOW A LASER PRINTER WORKS

Laser printers work by using static electricity. Objects with different positive and negative charges attract each other (like magnets), while similar charges repel.

1 The rotating drum has a positive static charge.

2 A laser beam shines on the drum, removing the positive charge from the places to be printed.

3 Fine toner powder, with a positive charge, is transferred to the drum by a roller, sticking to the non-charged areas.

Toner

Rotating drum

5 Heated fuser rollers "melt" the toner onto the paper.

4 Paper with a negative charge rolls past the drum, attracting the positive toner from it.

An inkjet printer squirts tiny blobs of ink from a print head, which moves quickly to and fro across the paper.

HOW A SCANNER WORKS

A scanner uses the same type of microchip as a digital camera—a charge-coupled device (CCD). It converts a light beam's brightness and color into electronic signals.

1 The document is placed face down on the glass.

2 One strip of the document is lit by a long, thin light.

3 An image of the strip reflects along a series of mirrors and through a lens that focuses it on the CCD.

The cover protects the glass plate.

4 The image of the strip is changed to electronic signals by the CCD. The light moves forward and scans the next strip.

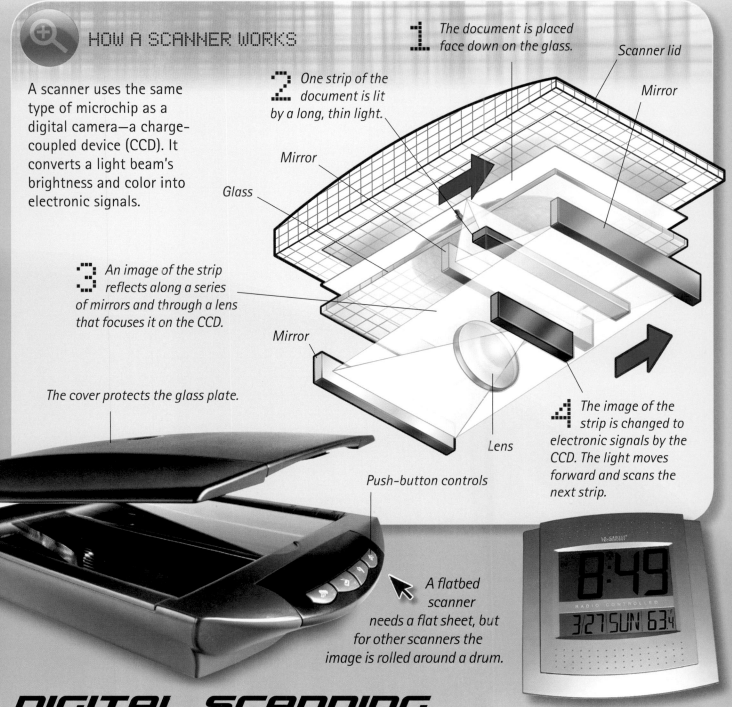

Scanner lid

Mirror

Mirror

Glass

Mirror

Lens

Push-button controls

A flatbed scanner needs a flat sheet, but for other scanners the image is rolled around a drum.

DIGITAL SCANNING

A scanner detects the color and brightness of each tiny part, or dot, of a picture or document. This information is turned into strings of digital code. The resolution of a scan depends on the size of the dots, measured as dots per inch (dpi). Smaller dots mean a higher resolution and show up more detail.

A desktop "atomic clock" receives the correct date and time by radio waves broadcast from a real atomic clock. The desktop clock can correct itself every day.

RADIO CONTROLLED

8:49

3/27 SUN 634

< 79 >

HOME SECURITY

Modern homes packed with expensive hi-tech gadgets can be kept safe and secure by other hi-tech devices. Sensors detect movement and body heat, webcams monitor rooms, and digital locks are safer and more adaptable than those with keys.

Digital locks need a code to open the door. For extra security, a scanner checks the thumbprint against prints in its memory.

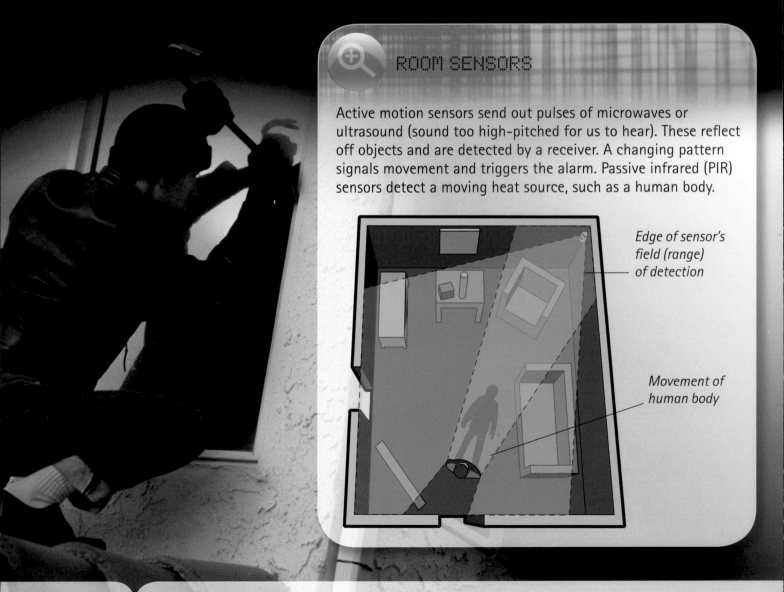

ROOM SENSORS

Active motion sensors send out pulses of microwaves or ultrasound (sound too high-pitched for us to hear). These reflect off objects and are detected by a receiver. A changing pattern signals movement and triggers the alarm. Passive infrared (PIR) sensors detect a moving heat source, such as a human body.

Edge of sensor's field (range) of detection

Movement of human body

This fireproof, flood-proof digital safe can be programmed with a security number, which can be easily changed after each use.

The code is entered using the touch-sensitive number pad.

The siren makes a loud warning noise.

Sudden light and sound are a deterrent to intruders, and are a cheap way of keeping buildings secure.

The PIR sensor can detect a moving heat source, such as a human body or vehicle.

RADIO ALERT

Security sensors may set off loud alarms, but if there's no one to hear, an intruder can quickly neutralize them. Advanced security systems are linked to the Internet, a cell-phone network, or a private security radio system. They send a warning to the owner or security staff, who can then find out which sensor was activated when, and even view the scene on a webcam.

The webcam scans the scene for any changes.

The wheels are driven by electric motors.

 GUARD ROBOT

As this guard robot moves around the house, its camera and sensors record room layouts and furniture positions in its memory. The "bot" is programmed to patrol the house regularly. Any suspicious changes will cause it to alert the owner by radio link, the Internet, or a cell phone.

< 81 >

HOME ROBOT TEAM

A robot never puts off doing its chores and keeps going until they're all done. Hi-tech houses may have a team of five or more domestic robots brushing floors, mowing lawns, and cleaning swimming pools while the humans relax.

The Roomba Scheduler can be programmed to clean at certain times. It automatically returns to its base to recharge.

ROBOT VACUUM CLEANER

The Roomba is low and slow. Powered by rechargeable batteries, it slides under furniture, along walls, and into corners. Infrared sensors stop it from falling down steps or stairs, and dirt sensors help it clean dusty areas more thoroughly. An infrared "virtual wall" beam (similar to the beam in a remote control) shines across an open doorway to prevent the Roomba from leaving an area.

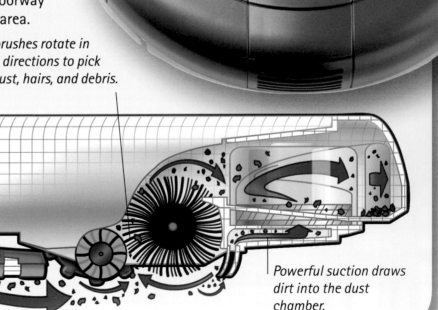

Side brushes clean along walls and baseboards.

Two brushes rotate in opposite directions to pick up dust, hairs, and debris.

Powerful suction draws dirt into the dust chamber.

A robot pool cleaner's tracks are powered by a type of fan blade turned by the water flow. This robot can climb up the pool's sides and automatically back out of corners.

POOL CLEANER

The latest pool robot will clean your pool from floor to waterline in about an hour. Roller brushes scrub the tiled surfaces while a powerful vacuum and filtration system picks up and traps hair, debris, and algae. The robot can also distribute chlorine. Like the floor-cleaning "bots" of the home, pool robots have bumpers that can sense physical contact and steer away. Some cleaning robots switch between a sequence of simple programmed routes, such as following a wall or moving in a spiral, and changing direction at random.

Debris collects in a mesh bag inside the cleaner.

Robot lawn mowers stay within a set area by sensing a magnetic field emitted by a special wire boundary.

 ## ROBOT CARE

Robots, such as Wakamaru, can be caring companions, especially for the elderly. They have webcam eyes and can speak approximately 10,000 words. If the owner does not respond after a certain time, Wakamaru can call for help on a built-in cell phone.

Wakamaru responds to questions.

ROBOT TOYS

The latest must-have toy robots are amusing and entertaining. But they also show off the latest in computer programs, speech recognition, sensors, motors, and other advanced technologies.

The infrared sensors respond to remote control.

Microphone "ears"

"Robosapien" refers to a series of programmable humanoid robot toys designed to imitate human actions and movements in ever-increasing detail.

Contact sensor on back of hand.

Cup holder for couch potatoes.

Articulated waist can bend and twist.

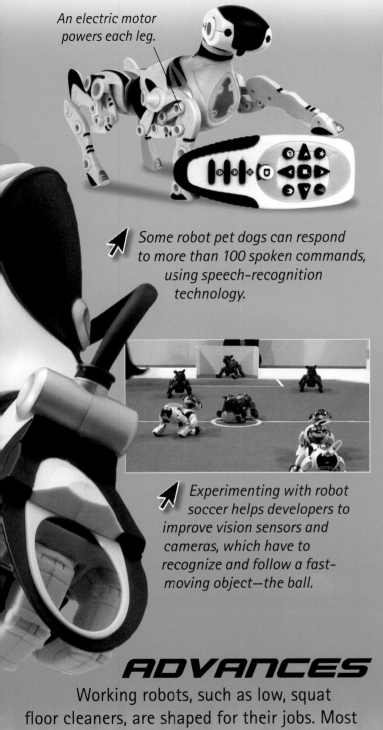

An electric motor powers each leg.

Some robot pet dogs can respond to more than 100 spoken commands, using speech-recognition technology.

Experimenting with robot soccer helps developers to improve vision sensors and cameras, which have to recognize and follow a fast-moving object—the ball.

ADVANCES

Working robots, such as low, squat floor cleaners, are shaped for their jobs. Most toy robots are designed to resemble people and pets and copy their behavior. This helps us relate to them as "friends" and makes play more fun. It also sets robot designers greater challenges to make the movements, sounds, and responses more realistic.

ONE STEP AT A TIME

One of our simplest human actions, walking, is very hard for a robot to copy. In trying to achieve this, scientists are developing better motion and balance sensors, and improved control programs and movement systems, such as electric gears and motors. These can then be used in many other types of equipment.

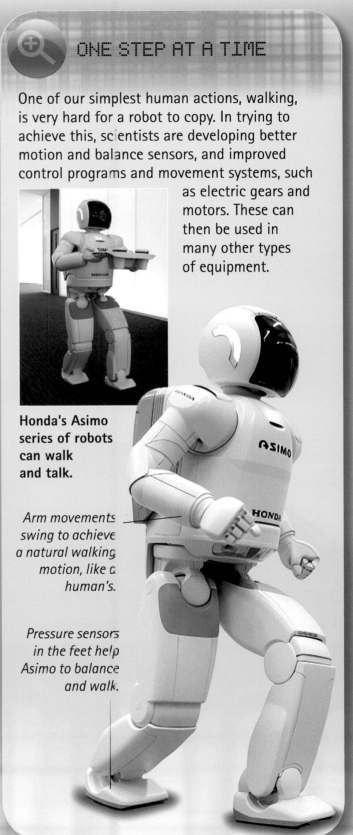

Honda's Asimo series of robots can walk and talk.

Arm movements swing to achieve a natural walking motion, like a human's.

Pressure sensors in the feet help Asimo to balance and walk.

JET SKI 96-97

SPEED AND MOTION

Much of today's most exciting technology is found in machines designed
for speed. Some forms of transport are convenient, cheap, or kind
to the environment. Others have comfort and style, while
a few offer the ultimate high-octane excitement. From
the sportiest car to the fastest train, there have
never been so many smart vehicles to ride.

STEALTH
FIGHTER
110-111

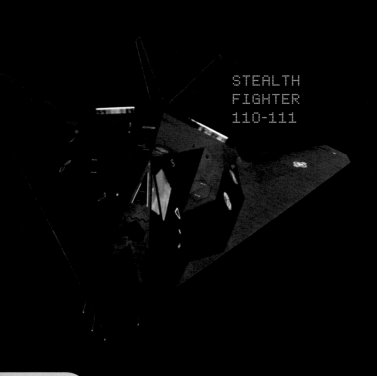

SPORTS CAR 88-89

MAGLEV TRAIN 104-105

Shanghai Transrapid

< 87 >

SPORTS CAR

In 2005, the Bugatti Veyron 16.4 became the world's fastest, most powerful and most expensive road car. If it breaks down, there's no need to call the local garage. Bugatti flies a team of engineers straight to the car, anytime, anywhere.

Only 300 Veyrons are planned to be built, with a selling price of about $1,200,000 each. The car can go from 0 to 60 mph (0 to 100 km/h) in less that 2.5 seconds and has a top speed of more than 253 mph (407 km/h).

Carbon fiber composite body

The luggage compartment is at the front under the hood.

Front underbody flaps close for top speed mode.

Aerodynamic shape

TOP SPEED

In "handling" mode, above 135 miles per hour (217 km/h), the car's rear fender and spoiler rise. Air rushing past pushes down on the fender and spoiler to keep the rear tires pressed onto the road for grip. Above 230 mph (370 km/h) the driver turns a special key for "top speed" mode. The car checks its systems, withdraws the spoiler, and lowers its body from 5 to 2½ inches (12 to 6 cm) above the ground.

INTERIOR AND SYSTEMS

The car's interior is leather covered, apart from the aluminum center panel (near right) and dashboard display (far right). About 8,860 feet (2,700 m) of cables, weighing 11 pounds (5 kg), link the car's parts. These include more than 100 sensors for conditions, such as tire pressure and satellite navigation signal, and 26 electronic control units with microprocessor "brains."

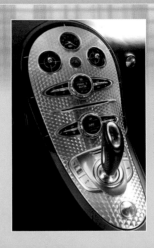

These dials show engine turning speed (center), road speed (lower right), and, more unusually, horsepower (lower left).

HORSEPOWER

The standard V8 engine used in many superfast cars has two rows of four cylinders set at a "V" angle to each other. The Veyron has two turbocharged V8s partly merged together to make an 8-liter "W16"! Sitting in the middle of the car, just behind driver and passenger, the engine produces more than 1,000 horsepower, about six times that of a standard family car. The engine drives all four wheels through a seven-speed transmission, with shifter paddles near the steering wheel to change gear.

From 1994 to 2005, the fastest road car was the McLaren F1. It has a top speed of 240 mph (386 km/h), and its 6-liter V12 engine produces up to 690 horsepower.

SEGWAY

Walking is "controlled falling." You lean forward, put one foot in front of the other so you don't topple over, and repeat the process. The Segway does the same, but with gyroscopes, a computer, motors, and wheels.

In some countries, Segways are used by security staff and police to patrol shopping malls and airports.

Handle for llifting the Segway onto transport

STEERING

X2s can race over rough ground.

The Segway is steered by tilting the handlebar stem to the left or right. This mimics the body's natural motion of leaning into a curve. Computers make the motor driving the wheel on the inside of the bend turn slower than the motor on the outside.

Secure grip handlebars

The Segway X2 is designed for rough ground, with splash guards, deep-tread tires, and a higher ground clearance (height of the main frame above the ground surface).

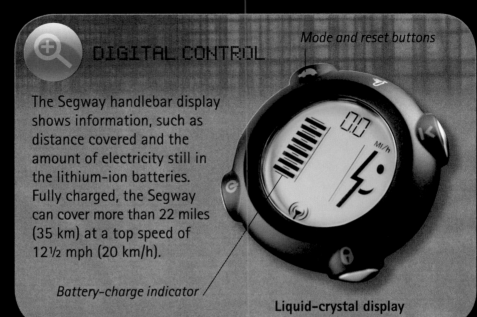

DIGITAL CONTROL

The Segway handlebar display shows information, such as distance covered and the amount of electricity still in the lithium-ion batteries. Fully charged, the Segway can cover more than 22 miles (35 km) at a top speed of 12½ mph (20 km/h).

Mode and reset buttons

Battery-charge indicator

Liquid-crystal display

GYRO AND BALANCE

The Segway is designed to mirror the process of human walking. To move a Segway forward, the rider leans forward and offsets the balance. The Segway then moves forward to regain balance. Changes from a balanced status are detected by the gyroscopes, and signals are passed to the computers, which then tell the motors to regain balance.

Segways are often rented to visitors for tours of cities and sightseeing areas. The Segway is a "green machine"—it is quiet, has no exhaust gases, and takes up less room than a car.

The thick tires are for rough terrain.

> **94** FUEL-CELL CAR **132** MOUNTAIN BIKE **216** GLOSSARY: GYROSCOPE

< 91 >

QUAD BIKE

A bicycle has two wheels. "Quad" means four, so a quad bike has four wheels. A combination of motorcycle and car, it has a motorcycle-type engine, handlebars, and suspension—and the rider should always wear a helmet.

A quad's suspension has long springs and oil-filled, pistonlike shock absorbers. The wheels can move up and down over bumps by more than 8 inches (20 cm).

 QUAD ATV

Quad racers splash through water.

Quad bikes are all-terrain vehicles (ATVs). They can travel across hard rocks and gravel, soft soil, mud, sand, and shallow water. The engine, its air intake and exhaust, and the electrical equipment, such as spark plugs, are positioned high up on the bike. This avoids water being sucked into the engine and damaging the circuits.

The Kawasaki KVF750 4x4 has a 750 cc two-cylinder engine. Unlike a car or a motorcycle, there are no gears to change. The continuously variable transmission (CVT) is like one constantly changing automatic transmission.

The throttle lever controls the engine speed.

Front shock absorbers

Wide tires have treads to grip dirt and slippery sand.

QUAD CONTROL

A quad bike's main framework, or chassis, is usually a cradle design made of steel tubes. Handlebar levers control the brakes. Some bikes are "2WD," with the two rear wheels driven by the engine. Others are "4WD," or 4x4, with all four wheels powered by the engine, and some can switch from 2WD to 4WD.

QUAD JOBS

Many quad bikes are sold as fun machines for leisure, but they can also do serious jobs on farms, quarries, building sites, and beaches. You can take part in quad competitions as well. Some are races on tracks or motocross (across rough country). Others are for stunts, known as freestyle or free riding.

Freestylers do leaps, back flips, and forward somersaults.

FUEL-CELL CAR

A fuel cell, like a battery, uses chemicals to make electricity. Hydrogen fuel cells use the simplest substance as their fuel—the gas hydrogen. In a hydrogen fuel-cell car, the electricity powers an electric motor to drive the wheels and run the car's systems.

Hydrogen is normally a light gas but, at the hydrogen refueling station, it is cooled under great pressure and becomes a liquid to save space.

Electricity from the fuel cell is stored in batteries and used for the car's systems.

Honda's 2007 FCX turns three-fifths of the energy in its hydrogen fuel into driving power. That's three times better than a normal gas or diesel engine. It also gives out no polluting exhaust gases.

A fuel-cell car's electric motor makes very little noise, and the exhaust emissions are simply pure water.

< 94 >

A GLIMPSE OF THE FUTURE?

Nuna cars, such as Nuna 3 (below), test solar panels that change sunlight into electricity for an electric motor, but large panels are needed. Toyota's single-person PM (right) has a rechargeable battery and electric motor, and a wireless system so the driver can talk to other drivers—for example, to avoid traffic jams.

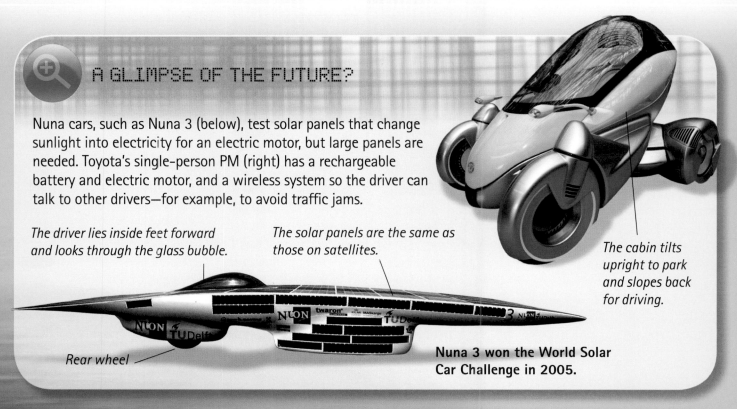

The driver lies inside feet forward and looks through the glass bubble.

The solar panels are the same as those on satellites.

The cabin tilts upright to park and slopes back for driving.

Rear wheel

Nuna 3 won the World Solar Car Challenge in 2005.

The Honda 2007 FCX's stack of fuel cells (left of picture) is about the size of a suitcase and weighs about 148 pounds (67 kg), which is much lighter than a gas engine of similar power.

CATALYST

A fuel cell contains a sheet of chemical substances called catalysts. Hydrogen gas flows past one side of the sheet, and oxygen from the air flows past the other. The catalysts join the molecules of hydrogen to those of oxygen to make water. As this happens, electrical energy is produced. One fuel cell makes about 1.6 volts, so many cells are joined as a stack to make powerful currents of 20 to 50 volts, depending on the vehicle.

JET SKI

The jet ski is fast, agile, and fun. Like a water-going version of a motorcycle, it skims across the surface of a lake, river, or sea. These personal watercraft are used by lifeguards as rescue vehicles, and by coastguards to chase modern pirates!

JET-PUMP ENGINE

The jet ski's motorcycle-type gas engine turns a drive shaft that spins a small propeller-shaped impeller, inside a tube. The impeller sucks water up through an intake grate that keeps out debris, and squirts the water out of the rear nozzle as a jet. This makes the craft react by being pushed forwards. Jet planes work in the same way but use air instead of water.

Kawasaki's three-seater Ultra 250X has a powerful 250-horsepower engine. Turning the steering handles swings the rear nozzle to the corresponding side, making the craft turn in the same direction.

Impeller

Driveshaft

Jet ski riders can perform leaps, side twists, nose stands, and even somersaults. They use natural waves or the wake of other riders to jump into the air.

Engine

Steering nozzle

Intake grate

The boat-shaped hull cuts cleanly through water.

SNOWMOBILE

Snowmobiles speed safely across snow and ice, powered by the same type of gas engine as in a jet ski. The engine turns a wheel on each side called a drive cog, which has "teeth." The teeth fit into slots in a flexible track—a loop like a tank or caterpillar track—on each side at the rear. As the track goes round, its ridges grip the snow and push the snowmobile forward. Small snowmobiles are used like motorcycles for one or two people, while larger ones carry more than 20 people.

To go around corners, the driver turns the steering handles, which angle the front skis left or right, and leans into the bend.

INTERNAL COMBUSTION

Internal-combustion engines work by setting fire to their fuel internally and converting it into motion through a rapid series of explosions. These engines drive all kinds of craft, from lawn mowers to trucks.

Most cars have front engines, with the internal combustion engine under the hood.

GAS OR DIESEL?

The two types of internal combustion engine are gas and diesel engines. A gas engine has spark plugs that use electricity to make small flashes of flame. These set fire to the mixture of fuel and air. A diesel engine does not have spark plugs. Its mixture is squeezed so much that it becomes hot and catches fire by itself.

A supercharger is a device that forces more air into the engine. The increased oxygen intake makes the engine burn fuel more effectively.

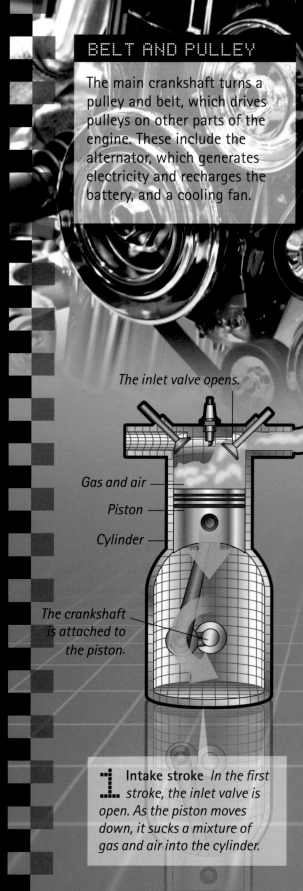

BELT AND PULLEY

The main crankshaft turns a pulley and belt, which drives pulleys on other parts of the engine. These include the alternator, which generates electricity and recharges the battery, and a cooling fan.

The inlet valve opens.

Gas and air

Piston

Cylinder

The crankshaft is attached to the piston.

1 Intake stroke *In the first stroke, the inlet valve is open. As the piston moves down, it sucks a mixture of gas and air into the cylinder.*

< 98 > ESSENTIAL FOR > cars · motorcycles · trucks · combine harvesters

FOUR-STROKE ENGINE

An internal-combustion engine explodes its fuel inside short, tubelike chambers called cylinders. Small engines on lawn mowers and some motorcycles have one or two cylinders. Large, fast cars and trucks have six, eight, or more cylinders for greater power and smoother running. In the most common four-stroke engine (shown here in sequence) there is one combustion for every four strokes or movements (up, down, up, down) of the piston.

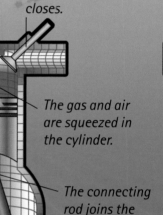

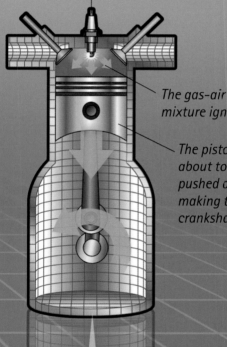

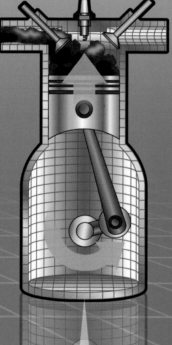

The inlet valve closes.

The gas and air are squeezed in the cylinder.

The connecting rod joins the piston to the crankshaft.

Spark plug

The gas-air mixture ignites.

The piston is about to be pushed down, making the crankshaft turn.

The gases are forced out.

2 Compression stroke *In the second stroke, both valves are closed so the cylinder is sealed. On its way back up the cylinder, the piston squeezes, or compresses, the mixture of gas and air.*

3 Power stroke *The spark plug produces a spark that ignites the compressed fuel mixture. This creates an explosion that forces the piston down again. This is how an engine creates the motion that keeps the crankshaft turning.*

4 Exhaust stroke *As the piston rises again, the exhaust valve opens. The piston pushes out the stale burned gases. The cylinder is now almost empty, ready for fresh air and fuel to be sucked in and for the cycle to begin again.*

AMAZING FACT > The smallest internal combustion engine is in a 0.1 cc model aircraft.

POWERBOAT

The fastest powerboats spend more time out of the water than in it! They seem to "fly," skimming from one wave to the next at 100 mph (160 km/h). The power needed to propel a boat this fast is twice as much as a car would need to reach the same speed.

P1 powerboats are the sea's version of Formula One (F1) racing cars on land. Their total engine size must be less than 11 liters, but that's about five times larger than a family car engine.

Propeller rising clear of water.

AT THE CONTROLS

In a P1 race the pilot (or skipper) steers the powerboat, watches for waves and dangerous objects, such as driftwood, and keeps an eye on the controls. The copilot plans the course by using the effects of wind and currents to find the shortest possible route. There may also be an engineer who checks the engines, their temperature, power output, and fuel levels.

Pilot   Copilot   Engineer

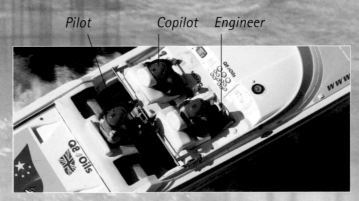

This powerboat has a team of three.

BUILT FOR SPEED

Powerboats are designed to "plane" across the water, which means the boat's hull, or body, rises out of the water as it gains speed. Having less of the hull below the surface cuts down the resistance, or slowing force, of the water. But the boat must also stay level and on course, and not go out of control. The hull is built from fiberglass, which is light but tremendously strong to withstand the hammer blows of smashing into the waves at high speed.

Streamlined fiberglass monohull

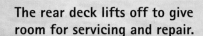

ENGINE

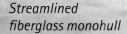

The rear deck lifts off to give room for servicing and repair.

Most powerboats have marine diesel engines in the back, either one, or two side by side. The marine diesel is very similar to a truck diesel engine, but instead of being cooled by air flowing past its radiator, water is taken in from the sea to flow past the radiator.

A powerboat's surface-piercing propeller is designed to be half in and half out of the water. This allows the propeller to be larger and turn faster, which gives more forward thrust than a totally submerged propeller.

SUBMERSIBLE

Exploring the ocean depths can be dangerous work. Manned submersibles with life-support equipment carry crews to study coral reefs or search for sources of minerals. Smaller, robotic craft investigate wrecks or study the geology of the seabed.

The Johnson Sealink Research submersible carries two crew and two observers and can collect samples from depths of about 3,280 feet (1,000 m).

ROBOT SUBMERSIBLE

An ROV inspects the wreck of the *Titanic.*

A remote-operated vehicle (ROV) is a robot submarine linked by electric cables to a human controller at the surface. It has cameras that send pictures to the controller, who steers the craft by signals sent down the cable to electric propellers.

The crew is protected behind a dome of thick, clear acrylic (strong plastic).

Video camera

Frame for lifting craft from water

LIFE SUPPORT

At a depth of 3,280 feet (1,000 m), the weight of the water above exerts enormous pressure. A deep-sea submersible's hull must be strong and thick to withstand this pressure. The craft carries air supplies and keeps the crew warm in the icy depths. Titanium-hulled *Alvin*, a 16½-ton (15-tonne), three-person craft operated by the U.S. Woods Hole Oceanographic Institute, can descend to 14,765 feet (4,500 m). *Alvin* found a lost atomic bomb on the seabed in 1966, discovered deep-sea vents ("black smokers") in 1977, and studied the wreck of the *Titanic* in 1986.

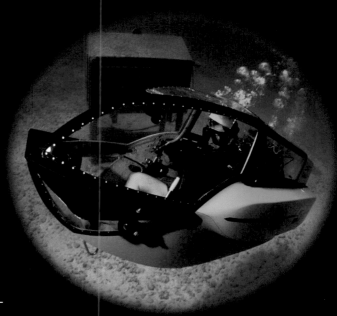

Divers use small submersibles as underwater taxis, saving time, effort, and air supplies.

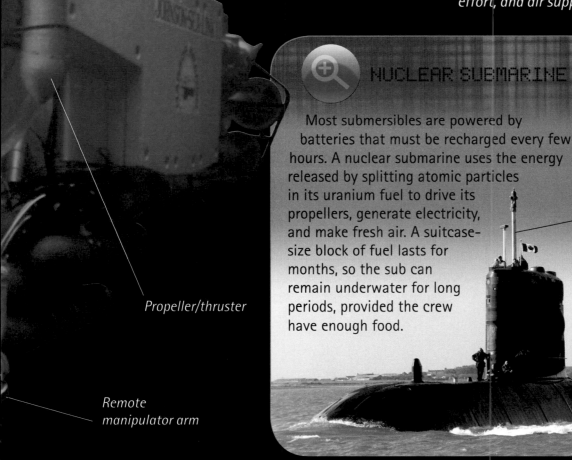

Propeller/thruster

Remote manipulator arm

NUCLEAR SUBMARINE

Most submersibles are powered by batteries that must be recharged every few hours. A nuclear submarine uses the energy released by splitting atomic particles in its uranium fuel to drive its propellers, generate electricity, and make fresh air. A suitcase-size block of fuel lasts for months, so the sub can remain underwater for long periods, provided the crew have enough food.

The periscope can see above the surface when the sub is below.

Submarines surface when safe to check their position.

MAGLEV TRAIN

"Maglev" is short for "magnetic levitation." It uses magnetic forces to make an object levitate off the ground. Maglev trains are quieter than wheeled trains, and can reach much higher speeds.

YAMANASHI TEST TRACK

In 2003, this Japanese maglev reached a speed of 361 mph (581 km/h).

The Yamanashi maglev track in central Japan is used to test new designs of trains, and how the track uses electricity to make the magnetic forces. The track runs for more than 25 miles (40 km) between Sakaigawa and Akiyama and has flat, straight sections, bends, hills, bridges, and tunnels.

In 2004, China's Shanghai Transrapid became the first regular maglev train service. It runs from Shanghai City to Pudong Airport.

The doors open automatically.

Shanghai Transrapid

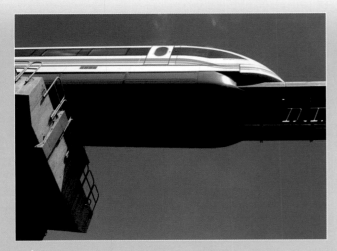

The Shanghai Transrapid runs across trackless bridges on its way to the airport, about 18½ miles (30 km) from the city maglev station.

Electrical magnets along the track push the train forward.

HOW IT WORKS

In the type of maglev system known as electrodynamic suspension (EDS), both the rail and the train exert a magnetic field, and the train is levitated by the repulsive force between these magnetic fields. The maglev track has electrical magnets that are switched on and off very fast, so the track and train's magnetic poles pull the train along.

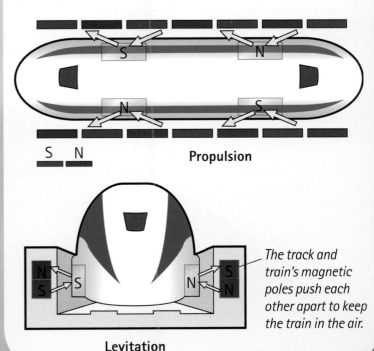

Propulsion

The track and train's magnetic poles push each other apart to keep the train in the air.

Levitation

PROS AND CONS

Maglev trains have no wheels or rails, so they are very quiet and have fewer parts to wear out. They produce less pollution than diesel trains because they use electricity. They do not suffer from rails slippery with ice in winter or bent with heat in summer, but they are very expensive to build. They also need certain features, such as emergency wheels, because if the electricity fails, the train would suddenly fall and scrape along the tracks.

GPS

You need never get lost again. Today, small satellite-navigation devices in cars, watches, and even cell phones can receive signals from global positioning system (GPS) satellites to pinpoint your location anywhere on the Earth.

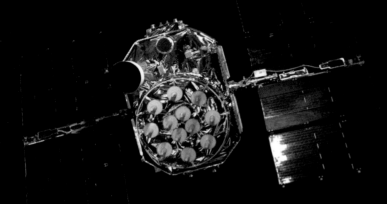

NAVSTAR

There are more than 30 Navstar satellites in the GPS, arranged in six main groups. In each group, the satellites orbit at the same height, but spaced apart, so they follow each other around the Earth. Each satellite is about 12,550 miles (20,200 km) high, travels at 8,700 mph (14,000 km/h), and makes two orbits every 24 hours.

Each GPS satellite weighs about 2 tons, with a main body as big as a car.

GPS receivers are now fitted into planes, as well as road vehicles, boats, handheld receivers, and wristwatches.

< 106 > ESSENTIAL FOR > cars · combine harvesters · jet aircraft

HOW GPS WORKS

The positions of GPS satellites allows signals from up to six satellites to be received anywhere on the Earth. The GPS receiver detects these and chooses the clearest ones. It then compares the signals, including the tiny time delay it takes for each satellite's signals to travel to it, which depends on how far away the satellite is. From these signals the receiver can work out its position on the Earth to the nearest 100 feet (30 m).

1. *Each GPS satellite sends out radio signals about its own identity code, its precise position, and the exact time to within thousandths of a second.*

2. *The receiver also knows the exact time. It compares the time delays from each of three satellites to find its distance from them, and so its own position.*

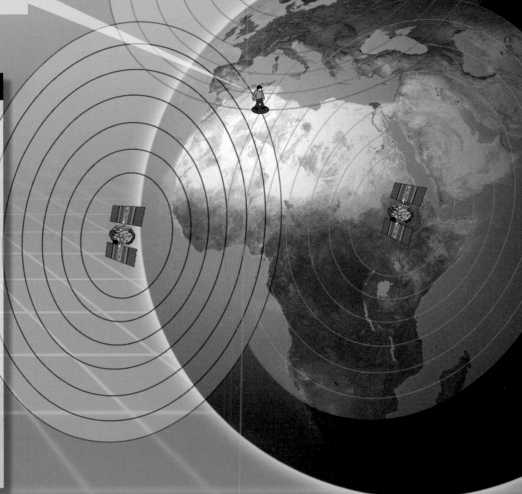

GPS satellite

GPS ON THE RUN

Athletes use GPS watches to record how far and how fast they run. The watch then works out how much energy the body has used, and whether the athlete's performance has improved.

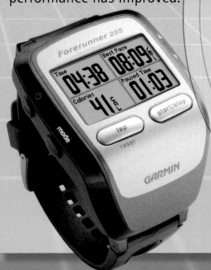

AMAZING FACT > A recent GPS gadget alerts drivers passing sites of historic interest.

‹ 107 ›

PRIVATE JET

If you're a movie star or an entrepreneur, your own private jet plane is the extravagant way to fly. This modern small passenger jet is packed with technology, from quiet and efficient engines to the latest satellite aids.

Layouts for the private jet cabin include soft leather seats, plenty of legroom, individual tables, and a luxurious restroom.

The Gulfstream 550 can carry 18 passengers at a speed of 560 mph (900 km/h) and an altitude (height) of 49,200 feet (15,000 m), which is high above most rough weather.

Rolls Royce RB710 turbofan engine

HOW JET ENGINES WORK

1 Spinning fanlike turbines suck in and compress air. **2** Jet fuel sprays into the air in the combustion chamber and burns with a continuous roaring explosion. **3** The jet of hot gases spins exhaust turbines, then blasts out of the back with enormous force, pushing the engine forward.

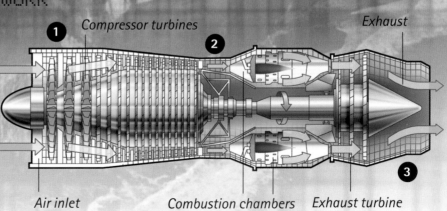

Compressor turbines

Exhaust

Air inlet

Combustion chambers

Exhaust turbine

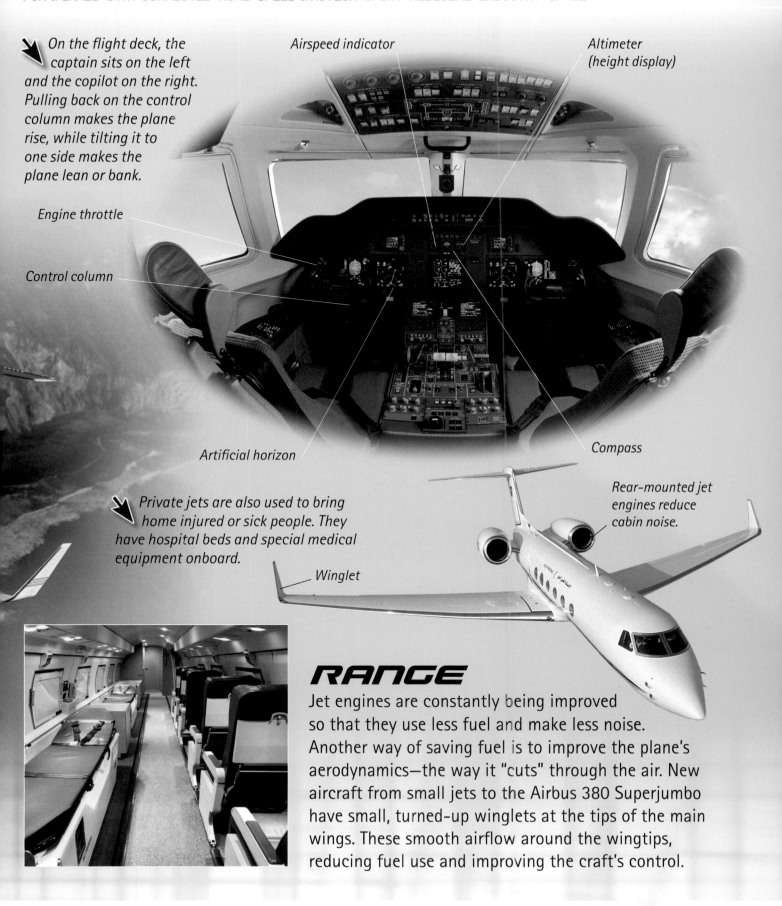

On the flight deck, the captain sits on the left and the copilot on the right. Pulling back on the control column makes the plane rise, while tilting it to one side makes the plane lean or bank.

Airspeed indicator

Altimeter (height display)

Engine throttle

Control column

Artificial horizon

Compass

Private jets are also used to bring home injured or sick people. They have hospital beds and special medical equipment onboard.

Rear-mounted jet engines reduce cabin noise.

Winglet

RANGE

Jet engines are constantly being improved so that they use less fuel and make less noise. Another way of saving fuel is to improve the plane's aerodynamics—the way it "cuts" through the air. New aircraft from small jets to the Airbus 380 Superjumbo have small, turned-up winglets at the tips of the main wings. These smooth airflow around the wingtips, reducing fuel use and improving the craft's control.

STEALTH TECHNOLOGY

Today's armed forces are always looking for new ways to conceal spy craft and weapons from their enemies. Modern stealth technology makes even large objects, such as planes and ships, difficult to detect by radar.

Ailerons make the B-2 bank left or right.

 The B-2 Spirit heavy bomber is the largest stealth aircraft, with wings 170 feet (52 m) across and a fully loaded weight of 165 tons (150 tonnes). Its "flying wing" design is very thin and difficult to see from far away.

Crew of two in cockpit

Four GE-F118 turbofan engines are buried in the wing thickness to lessen the noise.

WHY STEALTH WORKS

Radar works by beaming radio waves at an object, then detecting the bounced-back waves to find the position and distance of the object. A stealth craft's shape makes the waves deflect, or bounce away, in many directions, so very few reflect straight back. Also, the surfaces and paints covering the craft absorb radio waves, so any reflections are much weaker.

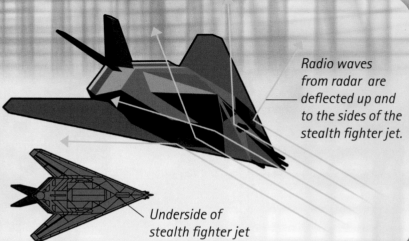

Radio waves from radar are deflected up and to the sides of the stealth fighter jet.

Underside of stealth fighter jet

LINKS 〈 **108** PRIVATE JET

V-shape tailplane (rear wing)

SUPERSONIC

Stealth craft rely on secrecy and surprise more than speed. The B-2 Spirit reaches 475 mph (760 km/h), and the F-117 Nighthawk 615 mph (990 km/h)—just less than the speed of sound. That sounds fast, but some jet fighters travel at more than twice the speed of sound—a speed that causes a sonic boom, which can easily be heard by the enemy. Also, the faster the plane, the greater the amount of hot gases blasted out by its jet engines. This heat can be detected by devices called infrared sensors.

Radar-absorbing paint

STEALTH SHIPS

Stealth ships use similar technology to stealth aircraft. Methods include a main hull made of carbon fiber, sloping panels, sharp angles to deflect radar, quieter engines, and a smaller wake—the waves from the front and rear—when traveling at slow speed.

This is the Swedish Navy's Visby-type stealth warship.

Jet engine air intake

The F-117 Nighthawk has a 43-foot (13-m) wingspan and two GE-F404 turbofan jet engines, one either side of the cockpit. Its shape and way of flying have earned it nicknames, such as "Wobblin' Goblin."

SNEAKERS 116-117

SPORT

To succeed in sport, you need to train, train, and then train some more. There's no hi-tech substitute for that, but the latest cool gadgets and equipment can help you get the most out of your body. From high-impact body guards that protect against injury to GPS wristwatches that measure how far and fast you go, sports equipment has never been so cool.

PROTECTIVE CLOTHING 122-123

SKIN SUITS

Human skin is tough and durable, but an extra layer of an advanced material can give a sports player the winning edge. Skin suits can enhance muscle performance and be extra-slippery for speed. Other fabrics can keep you dry even when you're sweating.

Several powerbands link sets of muscles to share their workload.

The powerbands store energy when stretched and release it to provide faster movements.

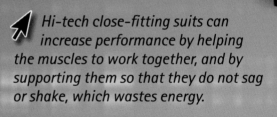

Hi-tech close-fitting suits can increase performance by helping the muscles to work together, and by supporting them so that they do not sag or shake, which wastes energy.

SMOOTH 'N' STRETCHY

The skater's skin suit reduces air resistance.

As the body moves faster, reaching speeds of more than 28 miles (45 km) per hour in speed skating, ordinary clothing causes air resistance. The elastane group of materials, such as spandex and Lycra, are supersmooth and slip through the air with less resistance. They are also super-stretchy so they don't restrict movement.

NATURAL SPEED

Our skin may seem smooth, but it has tiny creases and hairs. These slow people down, especially in water. Sharks and other fish have skin with tiny "go-faster" scales, which allow a smoother flow of water over the body. Sports technologists have borrowed this natural design to create swimsuits that increase swimming speeds by up to one tenth.

Fabric based on sharkskin scales

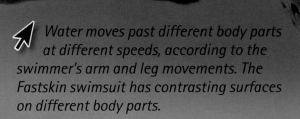

 Water moves past different body parts at different speeds, according to the swimmer's arm and leg movements. The Fastskin swimsuit has contrasting surfaces on different body parts.

NO SWEAT

Some fabrics, such as Gore-Tex, can "breathe." They let moisture from body sweat pass out, so you don't feel sticky, and they stop water from coming in. The cloth is a three-layer sandwich, with a middle layer of poly-tetra-fluoro-ethylene (PTFE). Its microscopic holes are big enough for air and vapor particles to go through but too small for liquids, such as rain.

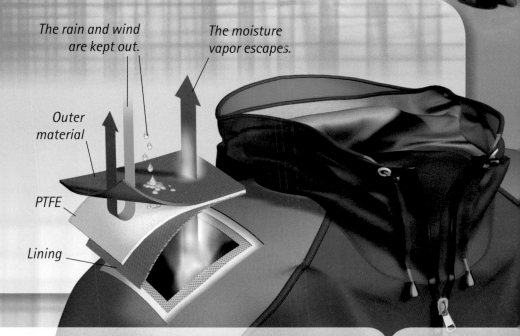

The rain and wind are kept out.

The moisture vapor escapes.

Outer material

PTFE

Lining

< 115 >

HI-TECH SNEAKERS

There are hundreds of specially designed sports sneakers and shoes, each tailor-made for a particular activity, from running to rock climbing. With sensors and microchips, footwear is now becoming "smart," too!

The molded sole gives instep support.

The Adidas_1 sneaker is a constantly adapting "intelligent shoe." A heel sensor determines how much the heel should be compressed on each stride.

The microchip and electric motor are under the arch.

Information is fed by the sensor to a microchip that continually alters the heel's cushioning, giving the shoe's wearer optimum support.

The magnetic impact sensor is in the heel.

The control buttons select a soft or firm heel support.

SMART SHOE

The Adidas_1 can record a thousand changes in pressure each second. It sends the information to a microchip in the sole of the shoe, which controls a small electric motor. The motor turns a screw that alters the shape of a cylinder in the heel to change its cushioning.

The motorized mechanism in the sole.

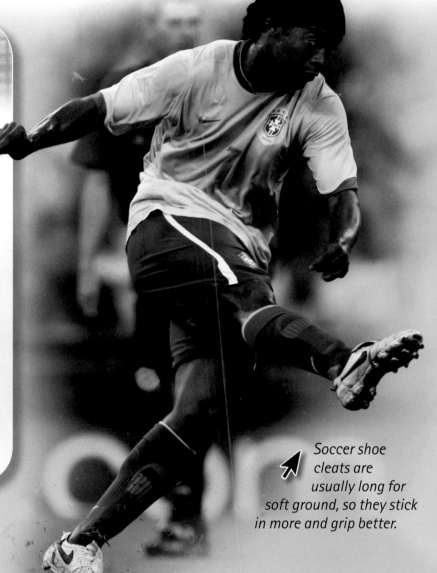

Soccer shoe cleats are usually long for soft ground, so they stick in more and grip better.

Mesh nylon provides breathability and strength.

STUDS

Players of football, rugby, soccer, and similar sports have to cope with ground conditions ranging from wet and slippery to dry and hard. They can adapt to these conditions by choosing different-size and -shape cleats, which fit into sockets in the soles. The cleats can be varied on each shoe to give more grip to the ball of the foot and less at the tip and heel.

Molded blades allow the shoe to twist if caught in grass.

ELECTRONIC COACH

Top sportspeople need to keep track of their performances when they are training. When human coaches are absent, electronic coaches can help record your efforts and make sure you're on course for gold!

Health experts recommend 10,000 strides each day. A pedometer fitted in a sneaker stores the number for later readout.

 ## PEDOMETERS

A pedometer counts the number of strides a person makes. Some have a small weight inside that swings to and fro. The Polar S Foot Pod uses an advanced version of this technology to record the speed, angle, and distance that the foot moves and sends this information to the Polar running computer (opposite).

A red light indicates that the battery needs changing.

The polar S1 Foot Pod is attached to a sneaker.

LINKS ‹ 22 MICROCHIP 116 HI-TECH SNEAKERS

PERFORMANCE

Electronic gadgets can store data about how your body responds to exercise. Heart monitors on the wrist or chest detect how fast and hard your heart beats, and chest-worn sensors trace how fast and deeply you breathe. The results are analyzed by a computer program to show how much energy you are burning, and even how much weight you are losing.

Heart monitor transmitter

The Polar Wearlink heart monitor has metal contacts woven into its material. These pick up the faint vibrations made by the heart's muscular walls as it beats.

The pedometer attaches here.

The pedometer detects how the middle of the shoe bends with each stride, as the foot comes down and pushes off.

RUN 'N' COMPUTE

The Polar RS400sd running computer, worn on the wrist, links to the Foot Pod motion sensor (opposite) and Wearlink heart monitor transmitter (right). The combined data are displayed to show how far and fast you run, your average speed, your heart rate, and to compare your latest performance to earlier ones.

The heart rate is displayed as a wavy line.

This running computer links in to the motion sensor and heart monitor.

< **119** >

WRIST GADGETS

The latest wristwatch computers can display your exact geographical position, altitude, depth, or speed. They can forecast the weather and even measure your golf swing. (They can tell the time, too!)

Presario 700

The Suunto watch display shows time, altitude, and a stopwatch.

This climber's Suunto watch includes a compass, altimeter, and barometer, and it has its own storm alarm.

North
330   30
300   60
Start Stop
West   East
20:26
2793 m
Mode
TIME [ALTI & BARO] COMPASS
View   Light
240   120
Log 1:46'32
SUUNTO
210   150
South

OUTDOOR ABC

Outdoor "ABC" wristwatch computers, designed for sportspeople and explorers, have three major functions. The altimeter (A) measures changes in height. The barometer (B) measures air pressure and helps to predict the weather. A built-in compass (C) shows direction. Heart monitors and GPS can also be added to some models.

A laptop computer can download the watch's information and display a map to show the route it took.

TRAINING WATCH

The Suunto X9i combines ABC functions with a GPS unit to tell you where you are, anywhere in the world, to within a few feet. Distance and speed can then be calculated and used by cross-country runners, cyclists, or skiers in their training programs. A port links the watch to a laptop, which can then compare the latest trip information with previous trips.

This screen shows air pressure, altitude, and temperature.

The watch memory can store up to 500 locations.

This port connects the watch to a computer.

The casing is water-resistant to a depth of 330 feet (100 m).

The lightweight GPS Pod clips onto your belt or jacket. It uses the Global Positioning System (GPS) to track speed and distance.

PROTECTION

Most sports come with some risks, but these can be reduced by wearing the right protective clothing and gear. Many sports specify protective gear within their rules; you cannot take part without it.

A football helmet's face guard shields the jaw.

HEADGEAR

The hard skull bones act as a natural helmet for the brain. But some sports risk very hard bangs, especially at high speeds, such as in ice hockey or football. A padded helmet of impact-resistant composite plastic is essential. The helmet fits snugly so the head cannot slip inside it.

BMX

Each sport has its own potential injuries. In BMX, riders tend to fall on their knees and elbows, so shaped pads or guards are worn. The bike itself can be padded on the handlebars and upper frame to prevent injury.

Ice hockey players, especially the goalie, wear a lot of protection in case they hit each other, the side barrier, a stick, or a skate.

< 122 > ESSENTIAL FOR > ice hockey · motorcycling · football

HOW IT WORKS

Most body protection works on a two-point principle. First, it spreads the force of impact over a wider area, using an outer layer of lightweight, stiff material. Non-flexible parts of the body, such as the head, have a tough, rigid covering. Flexible parts, such as the joints, which need to bend, use an ultra-strong fabric, such as Kevlar. Body protection also absorbs the energy of an impact by using an inner foam padding.

A flexible, shock-absorbing back protector can be strapped over the shirt.

Several inner layers absorb the energy of any impact.

Impact-resistant polycarbonate helmet

The shoulder guard protects the upper arm and shoulder blade.

These Lycra shorts and shirt feature removable armor.

SUPER SUITS

Allover protective suits have built-in guards over the body's knobbly, bony parts, such as the chin, shoulders, elbows, knees, and ankles. These guards are designed to spread the shock of impact to the surrounding suit, away from the bone.

AMAZING FACT > On a strength-to-weight ratio, Kevlar is five times stronger than steel.

< 123 >

AUTOMATIC REPLAY

In sports, the days of disputed line calls and dubious umpire rulings are over. Today, balls in tennis and rugby, as well as badminton shuttlecocks and ice hockey pucks, are tracked by computers.

The Hawk-Eye replay system observes a game of tennis. It uses systems that were adapted from military technology.

HAWK-EYE

ROLEX

OFFICIAL REVIEW

Tennis balls can be tracked at high speeds.

Systems used for tennis and cricket, such as Hawk-Eye, have high-speed video cameras positioned around the playing area to take hundreds of pictures per second. The computer tracks the moving ball from each camera angle, then combines all the views to produce the ball's path in three dimensions, accurate to a few millimeters.

Computers detect which side of the line the ball falls.

Melbourne

Each camera provides a different angle.

LINKS ‹ **16** DIGITAL CAMERA **18** DIGITAL CAMCORDER **74** AUTOMATED HOME

SPEED GUN

Speed guns, similar to those that check vehicle speeds, are used to measure the speed (but not the direction) of the ball in tennis, soccer, and other ball sports. They work by radar, sending out thousands of radio pulses per second. As the waves bounce off the approaching ball, they become squashed closer together, a phenomenon known as the Doppler effect. The gun's sensor detects this and converts the information to a speed reading, such as miles per hour or feet per second.

ELECTRIC FENCE

Body contact completes a circuit.

In fencing with swords, each fencer wears protective clothing with wire mesh woven into it, and a wire-mesh face guard. These form part of one electric circuit, and the sword part of another. If the sword makes contact with the opponent, this completes a circuit, turning on a light or buzzer.

These lines reveal a dead heat for fourth position.

The winner "dips" her shoulder to cross the line a fraction sooner.

Sprinters cross the finish line at speeds of more than 33 feet (10 meters) per second. A high-speed electronic camera takes over 2,000 images every second. The images are recalled one by one on screen, and lines drawn through the runners' shoulders to determine their positions.

SNOW AND SURF

As surfing and snowboarding become more popular, the boards get more hi-tech. This is because scientists invent new materials for other uses, such as in cars or rockets, and these inventions find their way to the board manufacturers.

A snowboarder gets to know exactly how the board will twist and slide by feeling its movements and responses through their feet.

"Getting air" (jumping or "flying") is an exhilarating experience.

Snowboarding pants have reinforced knees and seats.

BOARDS AND BINDINGS

A shorter board enables better jumping and twisting.

Boots are attached to the snowboard with straps called bindings. These anchor into metal fittings in the core, the main central layer of the board. Binding positions vary from person to person, depending on the stance width (distance between the feet), the angle of each foot to the board, and whether the boarder has his or her right or left foot in front.

Bindings hold the feet in a well-balanced position.

MAKING A SNOWBOARD

There's more to a snowboard than its size, shape, and colorful graphics. It has a specific thickness, and its weight is distributed in a way that makes it heavier at the front than at the back. It must also bend easily, flex in different directions, and slip across the snow. A typical snowboard has at least five layers, bonded together with advanced glues called epoxy resins, which hold the layers as they flex against each other.

Protective plastic top sheet with printed graphics

Layer of fiberglass

Flexible core usually made of wood, foam, or aluminum, or a composite material (combination of different materials)

Layer of fiberglass

Steel edges let the board dig into the snow while turning.

The bottom layer is made of an ultra-high-molecular-weight polyethylene material known as "P-Tex," a dense, scratch-resistant plastic that provides a slippery surface and makes it easier for the snowboard to slide.

Surfers add wax to the top surface of the board so the feet grip it well.

SURF'S UP

A modern surfboard is shaped by carving and sanding a large slab of plastic-like polyurethane foam called a blank. This often has a long, thin strip of wood called a stringer set into its length to make it stiffer and stronger. The shaped board is covered with layers of fiberglass material and epoxy resin glue, which set hard and smooth. Small surfboards called shortboards are faster, but they need large waves, while longboards are generally easy to ride even on small waves.

LINKS < 114 SKIN SUITS 122 PROTECTION > 132 MOUNTAIN BIKE 216 GLOSSARY: COMPOSITE MATERIAL

PARA-ACTION

Humans have always wanted to fly like birds, and parasports are the closest we'll get. Skydivers can swoop and glide using specially shaped sheets of hi-tech fabrics, and the latest wingsuits allow skilled skydivers to "fly" in a more birdlike way.

Headset radios inside their helmets let the skydivers talk to each other.

HANG GLIDING

A hang glider's frame is made of aluminum metals or composites, including carbon fiber. The wing is a fabric of polyester-like fibers (such as Dacron) or nylon. The pilot hangs beneath in a harness and controls the flight by moving the A frame to shift body weight and tilt the wing.

The pilot steers using the control bar.

PARA PRINCIPLES

Air pushes against objects moving through it with a force called air resistance. A large, lightweight, air-proof sheet produces a lot of air resistance and so moves very slowly, which is how a parachute works. It can never rise in the air, but it can drift down so gradually that it's almost like flying, controlled by pulling on lines (ropes) to change speed and direction.

Skydivers control their speed using their arms and legs. They can make formations, such as a circle, square, or cross, while falling at speeds of more than 165 feet (50 m) per second.

Wingsuits are sometimes worn by skydivers. Wingsuits inflate to form a wing shape, so the diver can glide through the air and even zoom upward, instead of simply falling.

WING 'CHUTES

The ram-air parachute has upper and lower fabric layers with strips between to form hollow cells. Vents at the front let in air, which inflates the cells so they form a curved shape like an aircraft wing. This produces a lifting force as it descends.

Ram-air 'chutes have a slower descent.

> 130 DIVING 216 GLOSSARY: COMPOSITE MATERIAL

< 129 >

DIVING

Humans can spend hours under the water using equipment called "scuba," or self-contained underwater breathing apparatus. This is a cylinder that straps onto the diver's back and provides a special mixture of gases breathed through a mouthpiece.

Scuba divers cannot talk to each other unless they have special microphones, so they use hand signals instead. Finger and thumb in a circle means "everything OK."

A mask keeps water away from the eyes and nose.

The air tanks are strapped to the inflatable jacket.

Fins propel the diver faster through the water.

The wet suit keeps the body warm and helps buoyancy.

DIVE HELMETS

Using scuba equipment safely requires knowledge and training. A much easier option is the dive helmet, which is simple to use. The helmet sits on the shoulders and air is pumped down a tube for the wearer to breathe and to keep water out of the helmet. A waterproof microphone and speaker are linked by a wire to the surface, so that the wearers can hear and speak to each other.

Dive helmets are comfortable, safe, and sociable.

AIR ON TAP

The average scuba tank weighs about 37 pounds (17 kg) and holds more than 530 gallons (2,000 liters) of pressurized air, providing a typical dive time of about 30 minutes. The air tank pressure is too high to breathe from directly, so it is reduced by a two-stage regulator. The first stage lowers the pressure from 200 times to 10 times normal air pressure. The second stage lowers it again to the surrounding pressure, which varies with depth.

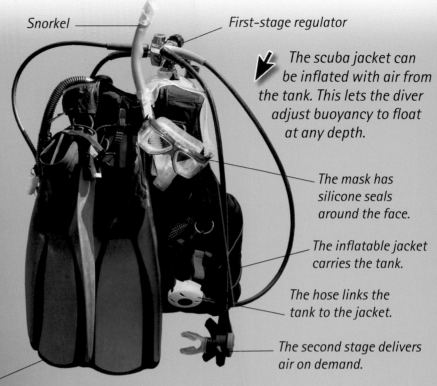

Snorkel ———————

First-stage regulator

The scuba jacket can be inflated with air from the tank. This lets the diver adjust buoyancy to float at any depth.

The mask has silicone seals around the face.

The inflatable jacket carries the tank.

The hose links the tank to the jacket.

The second stage delivers air on demand.

The rigid strips in the fins provide more swimming power.

 FREE DIVING

In free diving, there is no air supply or breathing gear. The diver prepares with special exercises and breathing routines, then takes a deep breath before diving—often for many minutes. Free divers undergo intense training to help their bodies exist on as little air as possible. The world depth record for diving without an air supply is 364 feet (111 m).

Pointing arms forwards reduces water resistance while swimming down.

The free diver stays close to the emergency cable.

> 216 GLOSSARY: REGULATOR

< 131 >

MOUNTAIN BIKE

The modern mountain bike is tough, rugged, and built to withstand riding over slippery grass and hard rocks. It has up to 27 gears, so the rider can climb the steepest uphill slope and then tackle a long downhill run.

A skate-style lid helmet made from hard plastic protects the head.

Flexible suspension soaks up the worst of the bumps. Some bikes have springs inside rubber casings. Others have pneumatic (air-filled) or hydraulic (fluid-filled) cylinders, as in a car's shock absorbers.

The shin guards protect the leg if the foot slips off the pedal.

The front fork suspension irons out the worst bumps.

Mountain bikers should wear protective clothing and guards. A wrist computer can be linked to the bike computer to measure heart rate and blood pressure.

Levers on the handlebars control the gears and brakes.

The tires have a knobbly tread to grip slippery surfaces.

The disc brakes give better stopping power than normal rim brakes.

Developments in alloys are making bike frames lighter all the time. The lightest frames, made from an alloy of scandium and aluminum, weigh less than 11 pounds (5 kg), which is light enough to carry on your back.

CYCLOCOMPUTER

The bike computer usually fits onto the handlebar and is linked by a wire to a sensor on the front fork. This detects a small magnet attached to a wheel spoke. The wheel size is programmed into the computer. From its clock and the number of wheel rotations, the computer can calculate the distance traveled, and average and fastest speeds. Some bike computers now also have GPS systems.

The digital display can be backlit for dull conditions.

The sensor detects each rotation of the passing magnet on the spoke.

FRAMES

There are four main materials for mountain-bike frames. Aluminum is light, strong, and stiff, so it lets the rider deliver more power to the pedals, but it can crack. Steel is cheaper and has a slight springiness but is usually heavier. A third metal is titanium, which is extremely strong and slightly flexible but very expensive. Carbon fiber is very light and stiff, but it is also expensive and may crack.

The angled windshield forces passing air over the rider.

SUPERBIKE

Few machines have more power for their weight than a race-tuned motorcycle. On a special track, the superbike can accelerate from 0 to 60 miles (100 km) per hour in less than three seconds, and reach top speeds of more than 185 miles (300 km) per hour.

DIGITAL DISPLAY

A superbike's display shows road speed and the engine's rotating speed in rpm, or revolutions per minute. This is useful because the engine's power increases with speed, producing the most power in a range of rpms called the powerband. The rider aims to keep the rpms within this range for the best acceleration and handling.

The displays are waterproof.

Dual display of tachometer (rpm) and speedometer

Front fairings (drag-reducing curves) form a "slippery" aerodynamic surface.

 The Kawasaki Ninja motorcycles are among the world's fastest. The ZX14 has an engine of 1352 cc (1.352 liters)—and can go from 0 to 60 miles (100 km) per hour in only 3.8 seconds.

LIGHT POWER

Many parts of a superbike are made of the latest composite materials. These contain various amounts of plastic, fiberglass, carbon fiber and metals, such as aluminum. The fibers are arranged in a crisscross pattern to provide the most strength for the least weight. The power-to-weight ratio of a superbike is more than 0.7 horsepower per 2 pounds (1 kg), or seven times more than a family car.

A superbike's tires have a wrap-around tread (the pattern of grooves). This means the tire still grips as the rider leans at a low angle around a bend.

A tough, streamlined helmet protects the rider's head.

The headlights turn with the front wheel.

Brake pad   Suspension   Disc

Tire

Axle

In a disc brake, flat, palm-size pads attached to the bike's body press on a large metal disc attached to the wheels. Holes in the disc let it cool quickly and stop the pads from overheating.

ULTIMATE RACE CAR

There are many types of racing cars, including sports cars and rally cars. Fastest of all are Formula One (F1) cars. These ultimate driving machines can reach speeds of more than 205 miles (330 km) per hour on specially designed circuits.

STEERING DISPLAY

F1 controls and displays on steering yoke.

An F1 car's steering is very different from a normal car. Many of the F1's controls and displays are on the steering yoke (control console). Each side has a gear change paddle, while the buttons limit speed in the pits, alter traction control to prevent skidding, and control a dozen other functions.

Airflow over the rear fender presses the rear tires onto the track.

Tires are changed according to wet or dry conditions.

Each F1 team has two drivers. Seen here are Lewis Hamilton and Fernando Alonso of the 2006–07 Mercedes-engined McLaren team.

Suspension connects the huge wheels to the chassis.

The front fenders keep the front tires pressed down for accurate steering.

TELEMETRY

More than 50 sensors and gauges gather information, such as road speed, engine speed (rpm), fuel level, engine temperature, oil pressure, and tire pressure from the F1 car. The information is sent by radio signals to the car's team in the pits (some of it is also displayed to the driver). This is called telemetry, which means "measuring at a distance." In the pits, each engineer or mechanic has a speciality area, such as braking, and uses the information to detect any problems.

The engine air intake is above the driver's head.

The telemetry aerial is in the wing mirror.

PIT STOP

A typical F1 pit stop lasts less than 10 seconds.

An F1 car usually comes into the pit two or three times during a race. The fuel hose delivers 3 gallons (12 liters) per second. Each of the four wheels and tires may be changed by a three-person crew. Damaged body panels are replaced, and the driver's helmet visor is cleaned.

The drivers receive information from the pit over radio links in their helmets.

DNA
FINGERPRINTING
142-143

MEDICINE

SCANNERS 140-141

Modern medicine is at the cutting edge of science—especially in hospitals, where laser scalpels are used for precision work and scanners can see inside the body to check for problems safely. Today, more diseases than ever before can be treated using the latest drugs, surgery, and hi-tech implants. Scientists can even extract our DNA to screen us for future health problems.

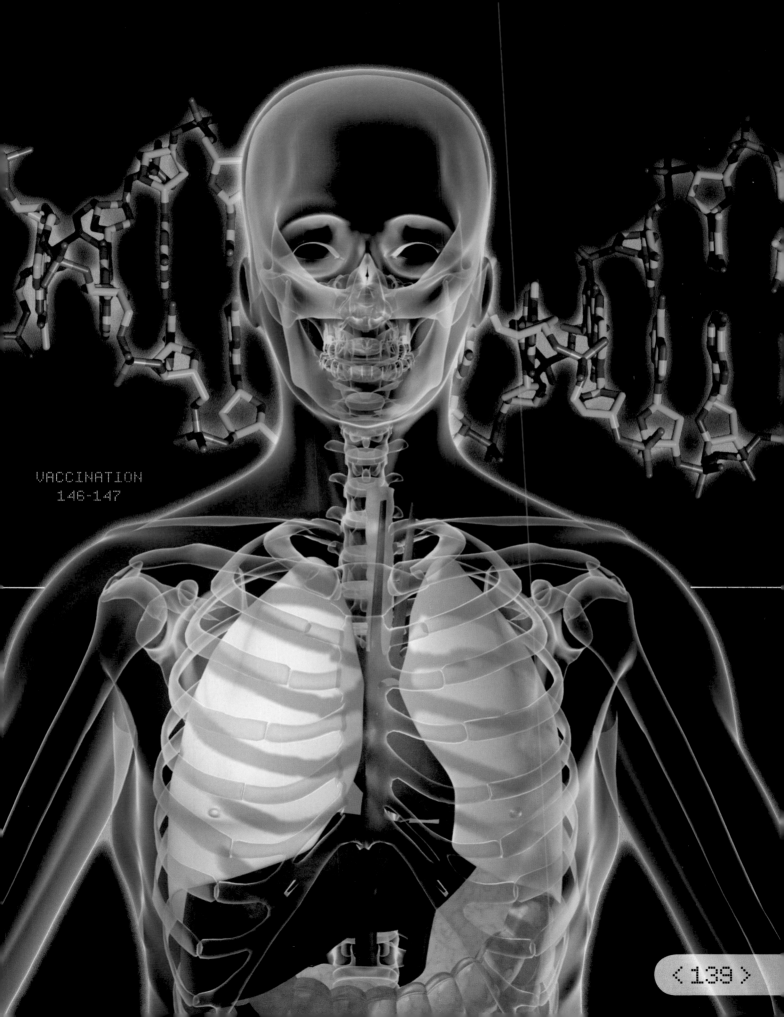

VACCINATION
146-147

SCANNERS

Modern scanners can produce amazing pictures of the insides of our bodies. Some take a "snapshot" like a photograph. Others take several real-time images each second, like a movie, to show how our insides work.

 A plain X-ray image is like a photograph of the body using X-rays instead of light rays. It shows hard, dense parts, such as bones and teeth, as white areas. Unlike the weaker but more detailed X-rays of the CT scanner, a plain X-ray does not reveal soft tissues, such as muscles.

Thicker areas of bone are whiter.

CT SCANS

Computerized tomography (CT) passes very weak X-ray beams through the body from different angles. Sensors measure the strength of the beams. Those that have passed through less dense areas, such as the lungs, are stronger.

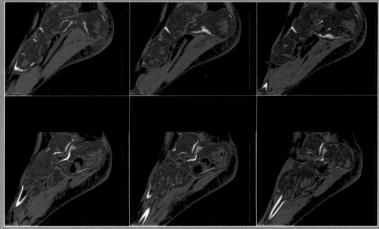

Each slice is combined to make a 3-D image of the foot.

"3-D" VIEWS

Scanners such as CT and MRI take a sequence of images as a series of "slices" through the body. A computer then puts them together to produce a detailed, three-dimensional, or 3-D, image of the body part, which can then be turned to view from any angle. The original scan is in tones of gray, but the computer changes these into bright colors. This makes it easier to identify problems such as lumps, which might need removing.

3-D ultrasound uses different angled sound waves to build up a three-dimensional picture of twins in the womb.

Ultrasound scanners send harmless, very high-pitched sound waves (too high for us to hear) into the body, and measure how these bounce back off different parts.

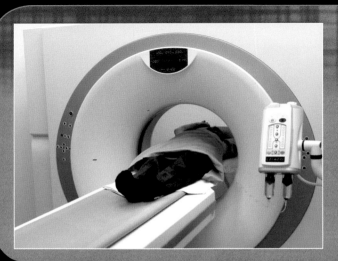

MRI SCANS

In magnetic resonance imaging (MRI), the body is put in a very strong magnetic field. This makes the hydrogen atoms in the body line up like tiny magnets. A radio wave is then sent through the body to knock the atoms out of line. As they line up again, they send out weak radio signals. The scanner detects these signals and uses them to build images of the body.

A patient lies inside the MRI scanner's ring.

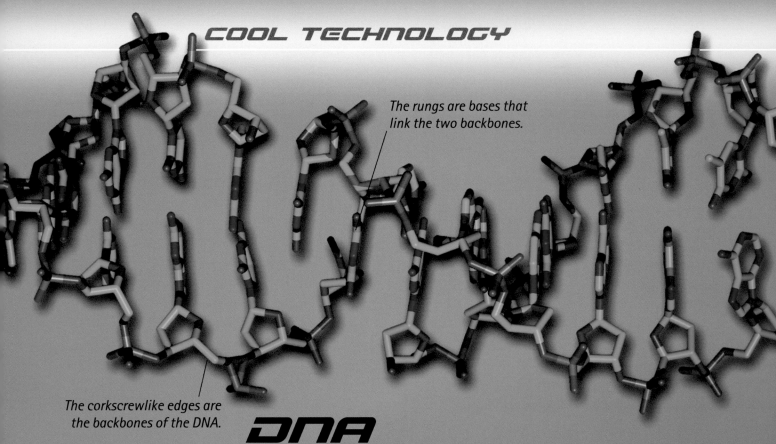

The rungs are bases that link the two backbones.

The corkscrewlike edges are the backbones of the DNA.

DNA is shaped like a very long twisted ladder, known as a double helix. The "rungs" are made from chemicals called bases. There are four different types of bases, and their order represents the genetic information.

DNA FINGERPRINTING

Deoxyribonucleic acid, or DNA, is found in all the body's cells. It carries the genetic instructions telling our bodies how to grow. Like our fingerprints, each human being has a unique set of DNA.

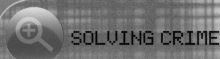

SOLVING CRIME

Even a tiny sample of body tissue, such as a speck of skin or blood, may contain enough DNA to analyze and obtain enough information to build a DNA "fingerprint." If DNA from a crime scene sample matches a sample from a suspect, then the chances are millions to one that the person was involved.

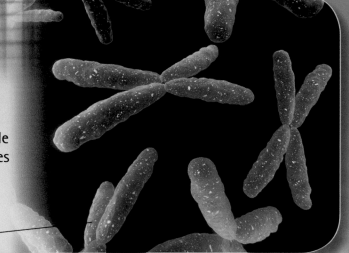

Each cell has 23 paired strands of DNA, coiled up into X-shaped objects called chromosomes.

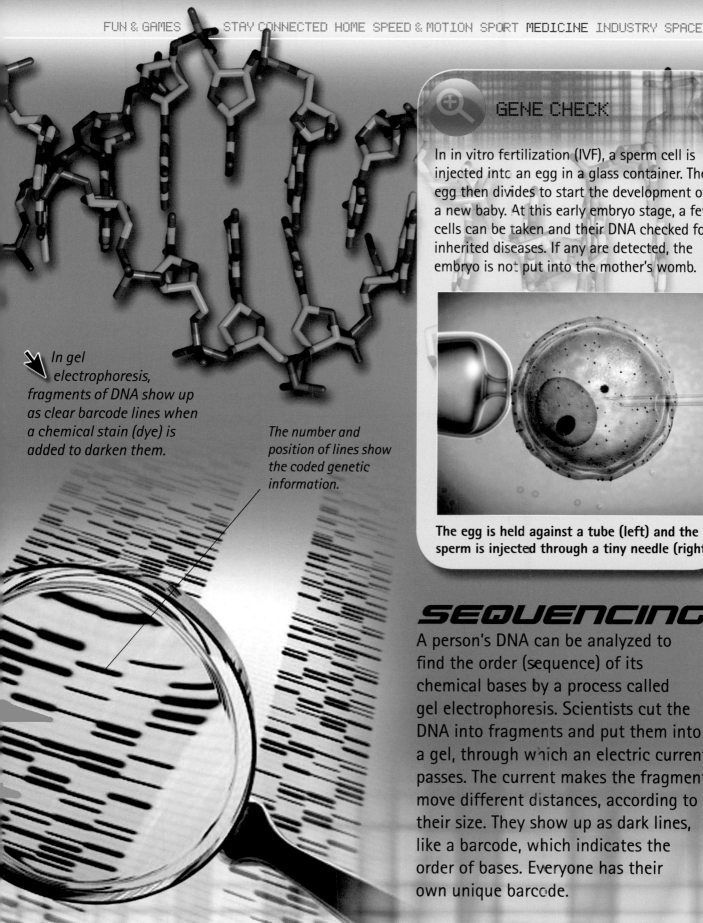

GENE CHECK

In in vitro fertilization (IVF), a sperm cell is injected into an egg in a glass container. The egg then divides to start the development of a new baby. At this early embryo stage, a few cells can be taken and their DNA checked for inherited diseases. If any are detected, the embryo is not put into the mother's womb.

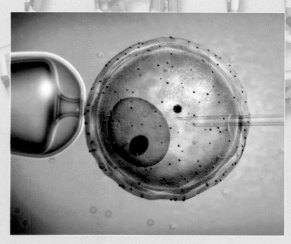

The egg is held against a tube (left) and the sperm is injected through a tiny needle (right).

In gel electrophoresis, fragments of DNA show up as clear barcode lines when a chemical stain (dye) is added to darken them.

The number and position of lines show the coded genetic information.

SEQUENCING

A person's DNA can be analyzed to find the order (sequence) of its chemical bases by a process called gel electrophoresis. Scientists cut the DNA into fragments and put them into a gel, through which an electric current passes. The current makes the fragments move different distances, according to their size. They show up as dark lines, like a barcode, which indicates the order of bases. Everyone has their own unique barcode.

SURGICAL CAMERA

Some of the world's smallest cameras are designed for seeing inside the body. These can be swallowed in a capsule or inserted into the body on the end of a device known as an endoscope.

A surgical camera inside its capsule can be as small as a pinhead. Because it's dark inside our bodies, optical fibers around the lens provide light so that the camera can "see."

The lens focuses the scene for a clear view.

DENTAL CAMERA

A small dental magnifying camera can get into all corners of the mouth and shows an enlarged view on a screen. This allows the dentist to see tiny details, such as cracked, broken, or pitted tooth surfaces, which could indicate decay.

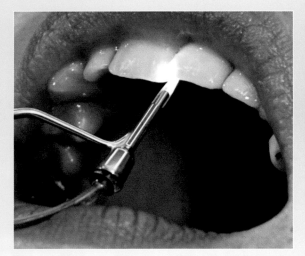

The dental camera uses a fiber-optic light.

A clear dome protects the lens and lighting fibers.

EYE INSIDE

A capsule camera is swallowed by the patient. It can find problems with the stomach or intestines as it passes along the digestive tract. A camera on an endoscope is guided by hand. The endoscope is a flexible cable. The camera has a lens to focus light, and sends it along a bundle of optical fibers. Each fiber carries light from a tiny part of the view, like a mosaic, along the cable to the eyepiece.

< 144 >
LINKS < **16** DIGITAL CAMERA **40** WEBCAM

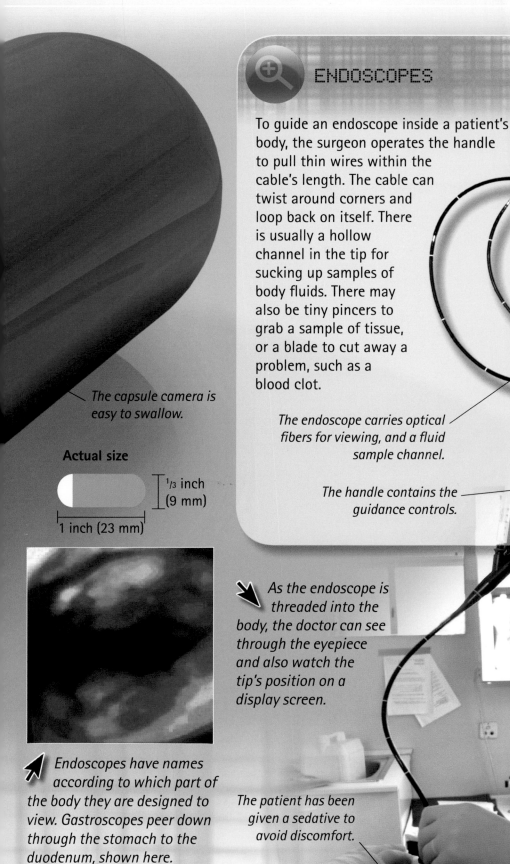

ENDOSCOPES

To guide an endoscope inside a patient's body, the surgeon operates the handle to pull thin wires within the cable's length. The cable can twist around corners and loop back on itself. There is usually a hollow channel in the tip for sucking up samples of body fluids. There may also be tiny pincers to grab a sample of tissue, or a blade to cut away a problem, such as a blood clot.

The illuminated tip is steerable.

The capsule camera is easy to swallow.

Actual size

¹⁄₃ inch (9 mm)

1 inch (23 mm)

The endoscope carries optical fibers for viewing, and a fluid sample channel.

The handle contains the guidance controls.

As the endoscope is threaded into the body, the doctor can see through the eyepiece and also watch the tip's position on a display screen.

Endoscopes have names according to which part of the body they are designed to view. Gastroscopes peer down through the stomach to the duodenum, shown here.

The patient has been given a sedative to avoid discomfort.

VACCINATION

In vaccination, a specially weakened version of a germ, or of the toxins (harmful chemicals) it produces, is put into the body. The body reacts by becoming resistant, or immune, to the illness without becoming ill.

VIRUSES

Most vaccinations are carried out against infections caused by the smallest types of germs—viruses. These are so tiny that a drop of water the size of this "o" could contain 10 million. Viral diseases prevented by vaccination include measles, mumps, and rubella (German measles), often treated with a combined vaccine called MMR, and also diphtheria, meningitis, polio, and influenza.

Several types of influenza virus cause different forms of flu.

Vaccines can be given quickly and safely by a "pen," which injects the correct amount of vaccine. The tip is then changed for the next person.

1. *The vaccine contains weakened germs that are grown in a laboratory. These cannot multiply in the body to cause illness, but they do carry chemicals called antigens that the body recognizes.*

ESSENTIAL FOR > disease protection · health workers · tropical travelers

HOW VACCINATION WORKS

Vaccination tricks the body into thinking it is being attacked by invading germs. The body protects itself by killing the weakened germs using its natural defenses, known as the immune system. The system then remembers how to kill that particular germ. Later, if the real germ gets into the body, it will be destroyed before it has the chance to multiply and cause disease.

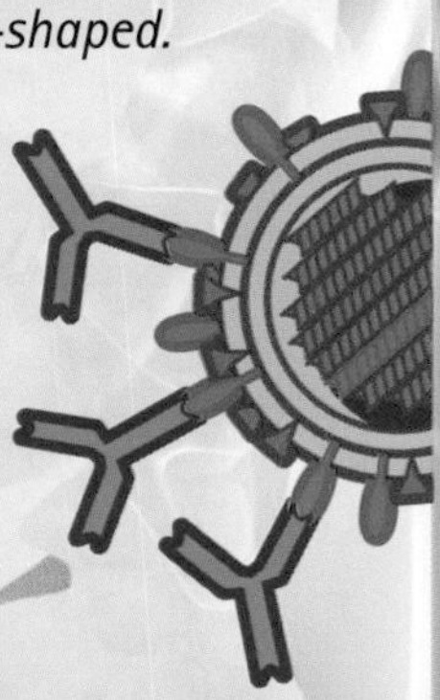

SMALLPOX VIRUS

In 1796, English scientist Edward Jenner successfully inoculated a boy with the cowpox virus. The aim was to prevent the boy from contracting the much deadlier smallpox, a related virus (shown below). A worldwide vaccination campaign against smallpox finally wiped out the virus in 1977.

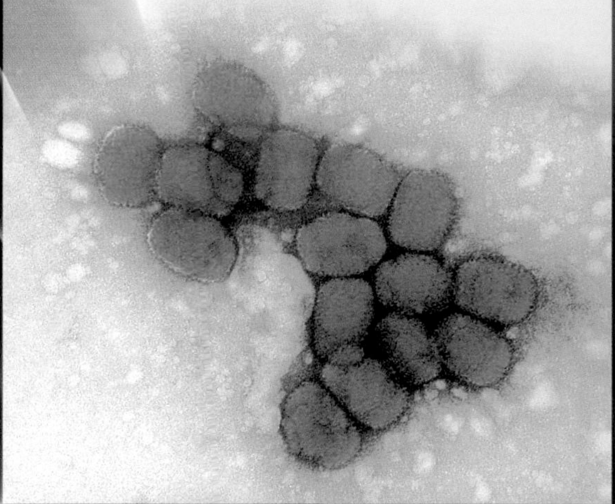

2 *The antigens are on the surface of the germ, forming its outer covering. Patrolling cells of the body's immune system, called T cells, recognize the antigens.*

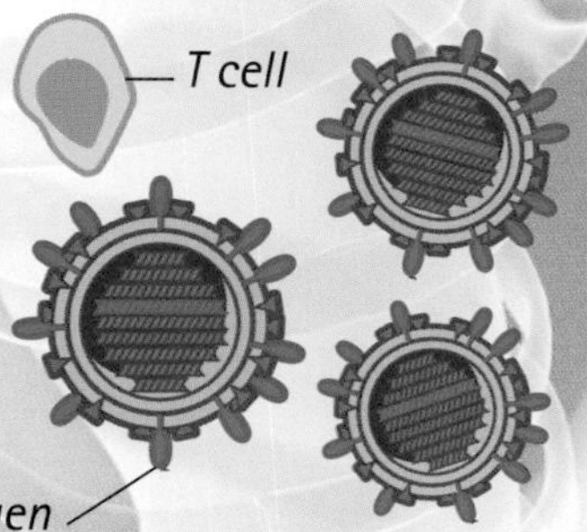

— T cell

Antigen

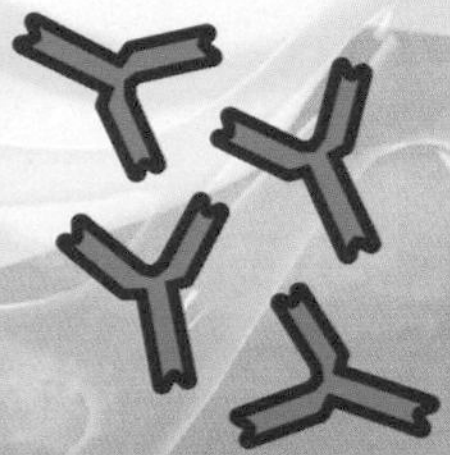

3 *The T cells tell other cells, known as B cells, to produce defensive chemicals. These are called antibodies and are usually Y-shaped.*

4 *The antibodies stick to the antigens, making the germs either clump together or break apart, and die. The immune system also has memory cells, which remember that type of germ and activate the body's defenses as soon as it appears again.*

Swiss Army knives come with a range of functions, including screwdriver, can and bottle opener, corkscrew, scissors, and tweezers. Digital versions include a clock, flash memory, and MP3 player.

EMERGENCY SURVIVAL

In remote mountains and deserts, help may be far away and a long time coming—so the best emergency equipment can be a lifesaver. Modern survival gear is lightweight and made from the latest durable materials designed to preserve life until aid arrives.

Cracking the outer plastic tube of a glow stick breaks an inner glass container and mixes two chemicals, which give off light for a few hours.

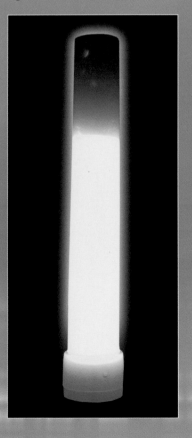

SURVIVAL KNIFE

The SL Pro 3 comes with flashlight and firestarter.

Outdoor knives, such as the SL Pro 3, have a rust-resistant, carbon stainless-steel blade that stays sharp. There's also a flashlight with a bright, low-power LED bulb and a whistle built into the handle. The slide-out firestarter bar is made of a magnesium metal alloy and showers sparks when scraped along the blade.

An emergency whistle is built into the handle.

The firestarter is being used to light kindling.

DISTRESS FLARES

A flare's intense light is visible for several miles.

Flares work by the reaction of two chemicals, or by combustion with oxygen in the air. Magnesium compounds burn in the air with a brilliant white light. Other metals are added for color—red is the international signal for emergency or distress.

TOUGH STUFF

Effective emergency survival relies on a combination of traditional knowledge and the latest equipment. Advanced metals and composites stay strong and do not rust. Artificial fabrics used for emergency tents and survival sacks or "bivvy" (bivouac) bags keep out wind and water, keep in body heat, and do not decay like natural fibers.

A durable nylon shell keeps out wind and water.

➤ *The clan tent is easily erected as a short-term shelter or bivouac. It's windproof and waterproof, with a superlight, foldout frame and artificial fabric.*

PARAMEDIC

In an emergency, a paramedic or emergency medical technician (EMT) will reach the scene in an ambulance packed with the latest life-saving technology. Failure could mean death instead of survival.

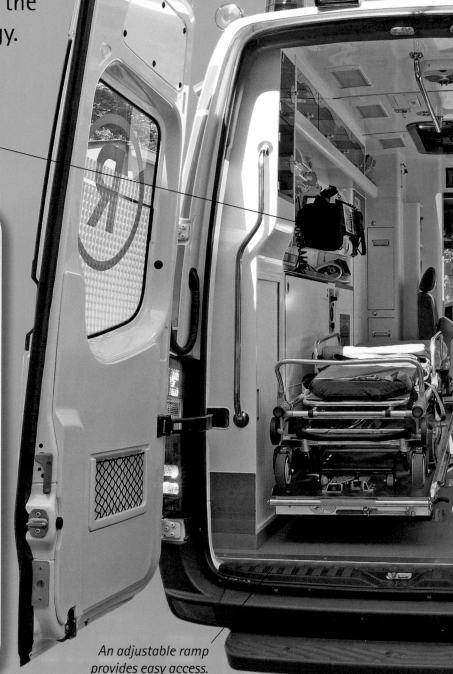

An ambulance carries a selection of fast-acting medical drugs, surgical tools, breathing apparatus, and other emergency equipment.

Emergency lights

A paramedic kit bag holds drugs and emergency equipment and can be carried from the ambulance to the scene.

 DEFIBRILLATOR

If a person's heart stops or goes into fibrillation (rapid, disorganized fluttering), the defibrillator can shock it back into a regular rhythm. Two electrodes are placed on the chest and a burst of electricity passes between them through the heart.

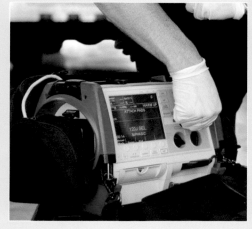

The defibrillator's charge is adjustable.

An adjustable ramp provides easy access.

This cupboard contains drugs, oxygen cylinders, and other equipment.

STRETCHER TRANSPORT

After a high-speed impact, it's best to move the victim as little as possible to prevent any further damage. To get the victim to hospital, he or she is placed in a spinal stretcher that holds and supports the back, neck, and head.

A special stretcher sled is used to carry a ski-injury victim.

ON THE SPOT

Paramedics or EMTs assess an emergency scene and its risks, decide who can be saved, and start life-saving treatments using lightweight, portable equipment. Common tasks include restarting a stopped heart, giving oxygen, putting a support collar on a neck injury, and giving medical drugs through an injection.

An air ambulance can travel directly to the scene of an accident, while a normal ambulance might be stuck in a traffic jam.

Height-adjustable stretcher on wheels

LASER SURGERY

Lasers have multiple uses in medicine. The intense, controlled energy of a laser beam can be used to cut, burn, sculpt, join, seal, measure, and identify problems. Lasers are safer and more hygenic than older methods using knives and scalpels.

EYE SURGERY

Lasers are ideal for treating the delicate eye tissues. For curing eye problems, such as far- and nearsightedness, the clear-domed front of the eye, called the cornea, is carved by pulses of laser energy that vaporize its watery tissues. Laser surgery can also be used to treat very delicate problems, such as breaking up a blood clot in one of the eye's tiny inner blood vessels.

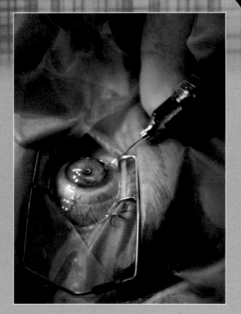

Laser surgery can reshape the cornea to help it focus.

A camera records the scene for training or for research.

A laser beam is made up of continuous light, or pulsed light in rapid, brief flashes.

The laser is generated in this barrel.

The surgeon can manipulate this medical laser either by hand or using a remote-control robot system with electric motors.

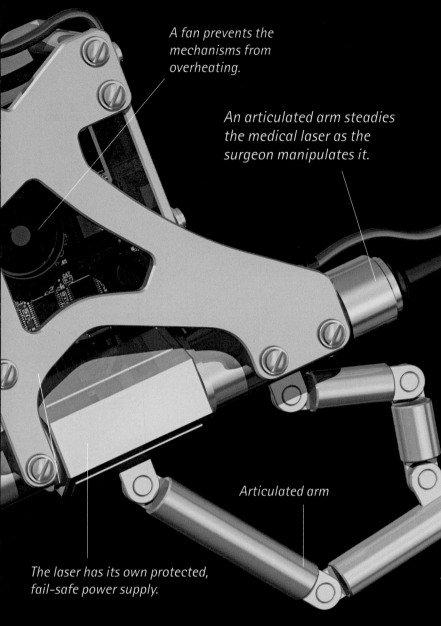

A fan prevents the mechanisms from overheating.

An articulated arm steadies the medical laser as the surgeon manipulates it.

Articulated arm

The laser has its own protected, fail-safe power supply.

LASER HEART SURGERY

In laser heart surgery, a beam can travel down a catheter—a long flexible tube inserted into the body. An ultraviolet chemical laser called an excimer is used to break up clots in a small blood vessel, or to "drill" holes into weak heart muscle in order to encourage blood supply to the muscle and make it stronger.

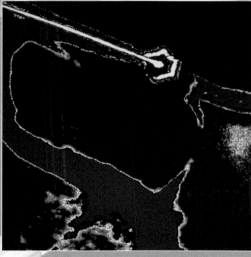

Here, a laser is vaporizing a blood clot in a coronary (heart) artery.

Dental lasers are used to kill bacteria, reshape gums, and sculpt teeth. The beam's heat seals off tiny blood vessels as it cuts through them, which reduces bleeding.

LASER TYPES

More than ten types of lasers are used in medicine, depending on the body tissue (ranging from hard bone to blood). Each type uses a different power and wavelength (color) of light. The power and wavelength depend on the "active medium" that makes the beam. The most commonly used is the carbon dioxide laser, which works like a scalpel. It is used for certain tasks, such as removing birthmarks.

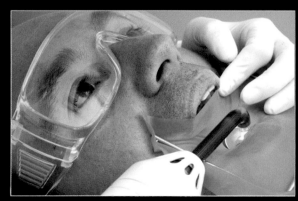

SMART IMPLANTS

Smart implants are devices inserted into the body to help people see and hear properly. A cochlear implant in the ear, for example, turns sound-wave vibrations into electrical nerve signals passed to the brain.

A transmitter sends out short-range radio signals.

Microphone

 ## COCHLEAR IMPLANTS

Some people who cannot hear have a problem with the tiny bones that carry sound vibrations within the ear. A cochlear implant bypasses the bones and sends electronic signals to the brain via the inner ear. The implant has two main parts: the microphone and transmitter, and the receiver with its electrode wires.

Transmitter

Receiver

Microphone clipped behind ear

Electrode wires implanted in skin

Electrodes are implanted in the cochlea and make its nerve receptors send signals to the brain.

► *The microphone and battery pack clip behind the ear. The microphone turns sound waves into electrical signals for the small radio transmitter.*

► *The receiver detects the radio waves through the skin and converts them to electrical signals for the cochlea.*

The receiver has a wire coil aerial.

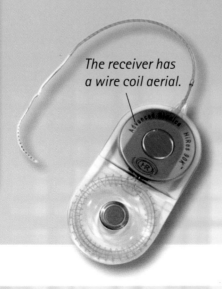

ARTIFICIAL SIGHT

A retinal implant works in a similar way to a cochlear implant, in this case delivering signals to the light-sensitive layer lining the back of the eyeball. However, the technology is still in development. Once perfected it will not only provide sight, but could also be used in other areas, such as personal computing and robotics.

The retina inside the eye has more than 120 million light-sensitive cells, but patches of these may die if their delicate blood vessels get blocked, for example, by a blood clot.

4 *The retinal implant emits pulses that travel along the optic nerve to the brain.*

Retina

3 *The receiver sends signals through a tiny cable to an electrode panel implanted on the back wall of the eye (retina).*

1 *A camera on the glasses captures images and sends the data to the microprocessor.*

Implanted cable

Receiver

Sight with a retinal implant is not much like normal vision. Users will see a scoreboard-type image made up of bright points of light. Over time, scientists will probably find ways of refining the vision.

2 *The microprocessor converts the data to electronic signals and transmits them to the receiver.*

Microprocessor

< 155 >

BODY TECHNOLOGY

Artificial body parts have come a long way since wooden false teeth. Today's prosthetic hands can pick up a pin, and an artificial heart has a life-giving beat.

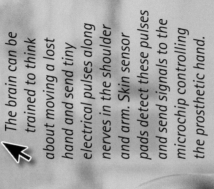

The brain can be trained to think about moving a lost hand and send tiny electrical pulses along nerves in the shoulder and arm. Skin sensor pads detect these pulses and send signals to the microchip controlling the prosthetic hand.

Running "blades" called Cheetahs are made from a carbon-fiber composite and are specially designed for athletes who have lost part of their legs.

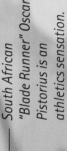

South African "Blade Runner" Oscar Pistorius is an athletics sensation.

ELECTRONIC HEART

An artificial heart can take over from a failing heart until a transplant is available. Its electric motor spins up to 8,000 times per minute and drives a hydraulic pump that moves the blood. Sensors on an electronic controller monitor the body's activity and speed up the motor during physical action. The motor's batteries are recharged wirelessly, so there are no tubes or wires into the body.

A made-to-measure holster straps onto the leg stump.

The blade bends as it hits the ground, then releases the energy to push the athlete onto the next stride.

Running blades are lighter than real feet.

A heart-lung bypass machine takes over while an artificial heart is connected into the blood system.

HELPING HAND

A real hand contains nerves that gather information about touch and movement, and feed it back to the brain. An artificial hand has a similar feedback system, using touch and pressure sensors in the fingertips that feed back to a device that presses on the skin of the wearer's arm.

A motor-and-gear system help to bend each finger.

BODY ENGINEERS

Body tissues contain nerves that carry information about movement to the body's muscles, which in turn push, pull, and lift the bones. Prosthesis engineers design artificial versions of these structures. A microchip "mini-brain" sends electronic information along wires to electric motors, which push and pull skeletal parts made from strong, lightweight materials, such as carbon fiber and metal alloys.

LINKS ⟨ **154** SMART IMPLANTS ⟩ **166** ROBOT WORKER **216** GLOSSARY: PROSTHESIS

ROBOT SURGERY

Some operations are so tricky that only a few specially trained surgeons can do them well or give the best advice. But what if the surgeon and patient are half a world apart? One answer is telesurgery using a robot surgeon.

The anesthetist monitors the patient's condition.

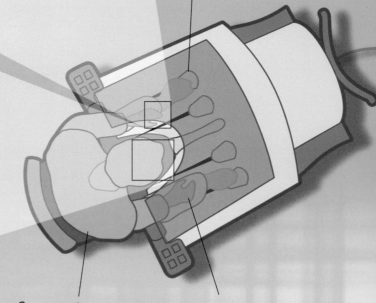

The surgeon's EndoWrist console contains two sets of control mechanisms with multiple levers and joints that can move in all directions. These movements are then coded into signals, which are sent to the robot surgeon.

Foot pedals reposition the image.

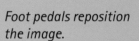

The surgeon watches the operation on special three-dimensional goggles. Foot pedals adjust the cameras so the surgeon can make the view zoom in or out, or move left, right, up, or down.

Surgeon at operative console

The surgeon's hand movements are precisely replicated by the EndoWrist instruments.

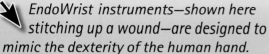

EndoWrist instruments—shown here stitching up a wound—are designed to mimic the dexterity of the human hand.

REMOTE ROBOT

Telesurgery or remote robotic surgery refers to medical operations carried out over a distance. The surgeon's controls are packed with movement and pressure sensors that precisely detect hand and finger movements and send the information via an Internet-like link to a robotic surgeon, which reproduces the movements on the patient. Cameras monitor the operation, sending the information back to the surgeon to follow on a screen or headset.

Image processing equipment

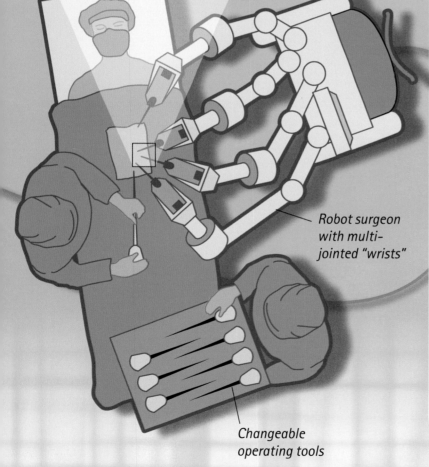

Robot surgeon with multi-jointed "wrists"

Changeable operating tools

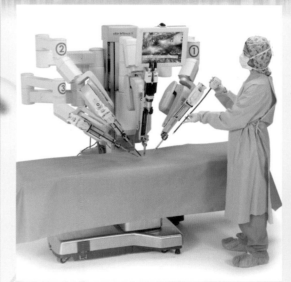

ROBOT HANDS

Remote-controlled hands ready to operate.

The robot surgeon has four or more sets of "hands" with detachable tips. There are different tip designs for cutting, holding back the skin and organs, pressing, and other tasks. The assistant surgeon and nursing staff change the tips when required, as they check the patient and talk "down the line" to the main surgeon.

GERM KILLERS

White blood cells are cells in the body's immune system that defend the body against germs, disease, and foreign materials. Some people have faulty immune systems where the white cells do not work properly—in these cases, medical nanobots could do the job for them, injecting special chemicals to kill the germs.

A nanobot checks a red blood cell for germs inside.

A nanobot locks onto the chemical covering of an invading germ and destroys it.

Some microscopic germs, such as those that cause malaria, hide and multiply inside red blood cells. Medical nanobots could find and destroy the infected red cells and their germs.

This red-cell-sized nanobot is about one-hundredth of a millimeter—a tiny fraction of an inch long.

NANOMEDICINE

Nanotechnology involves devices built at the scale of individual atoms and molecules, which are much smaller than the body's microscopic cells. Future medical "nanobots" could be small enough to float in the blood and even get into body cells.

The nanomask has filter holes more than ten times smaller than those in a normal medical mask. These let through air but keep out the smallest types of floating germs.

TINY HELPERS

Nanoscale robots could carry out many tasks around the body. They could detect chemicals released by blood clots and break these apart in places where they could be dangerous, such as in the blood vessels of the heart or brain. Nanocapsules could contain tiny amounts of medical drugs, which they release only when they get to the body part that needs the treatment.

 QUANTUM DOTS

Quantum dots are approximately 10 nanometers across—10,000 would fit on this period. Each contains a light-producing substance, such as cadmium selenide. Dots can be made that attach to certain body substances, such as the germ-killing antibodies of the immune system. Scientists can then see how the antibodies work by following their glows under a microscope.

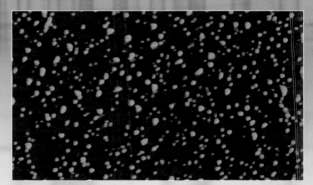

The glow of quantum dots under a microscope.

PERSONAL CARE

While surgery can achieve amazing results, people can also stay healthy and pain-free with smart personal care gadgets, and use portable monitors to check their bodies regularly for any health problems.

Vertebra in the spinal column

Electrodes are implanted in the nerves of the spinal cord.

Electrical wires connect to the electrodes.

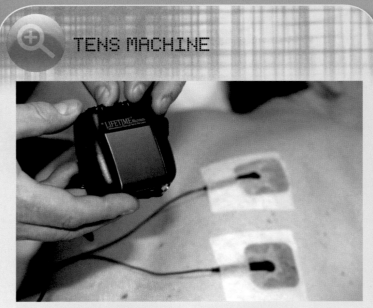

TENS MACHINE

TENS is usually applied for 15–20 minutes at a time.

Some people experience pain relief from transcutaneous ("across skin") electrical nerve stimulation, or TENS. This small machine sends electrical signals to electrodes in sticky pads placed on the skin. As electricity passes between the pads, it helps to block the pain nerve signals.

To block out severe long-term pain, a spinal cord stimulator can be inserted into the backbone to deliver small electrical pulses to the body's main nerve.

SYS means systolic blood pressure—the pressure when the heart contracts.

Wrist monitors have sensors that press on the wrist's main artery. Its rate of pulsation (bulging) shows the heart's speed in beats per minute. The force of each pulsation shows blood pressure.

HEARTBEAT

A healthy heart is vital for our well-being. A portable heart monitor, which can measure blood pressure and pulse, is essential for anyone with a history of cardio (heart) problems. The faster the pulse rate and blood pressure return to normal after activity, the healthier the heart. Athletes also use heart monitors to measure their fitness after intense training.

DIA means diastolic blood pressure—the pressure when the heart relaxes between beats.

MASSAGE MACHINES

Squeezing, stroking, and kneading body parts can relax tense muscles, improve blood flow, and ease stiff joints. Computer-controlled massagers have various speeds and settings, from gentle to powerful. Sensors monitor the pressure they apply and adjust it for the best effect.

This luxurious massage machine squeezes and kneads the foot muscles.

▷ **216** GLOSSARY: ELECTRODE

ROBOT WORKER
166-167

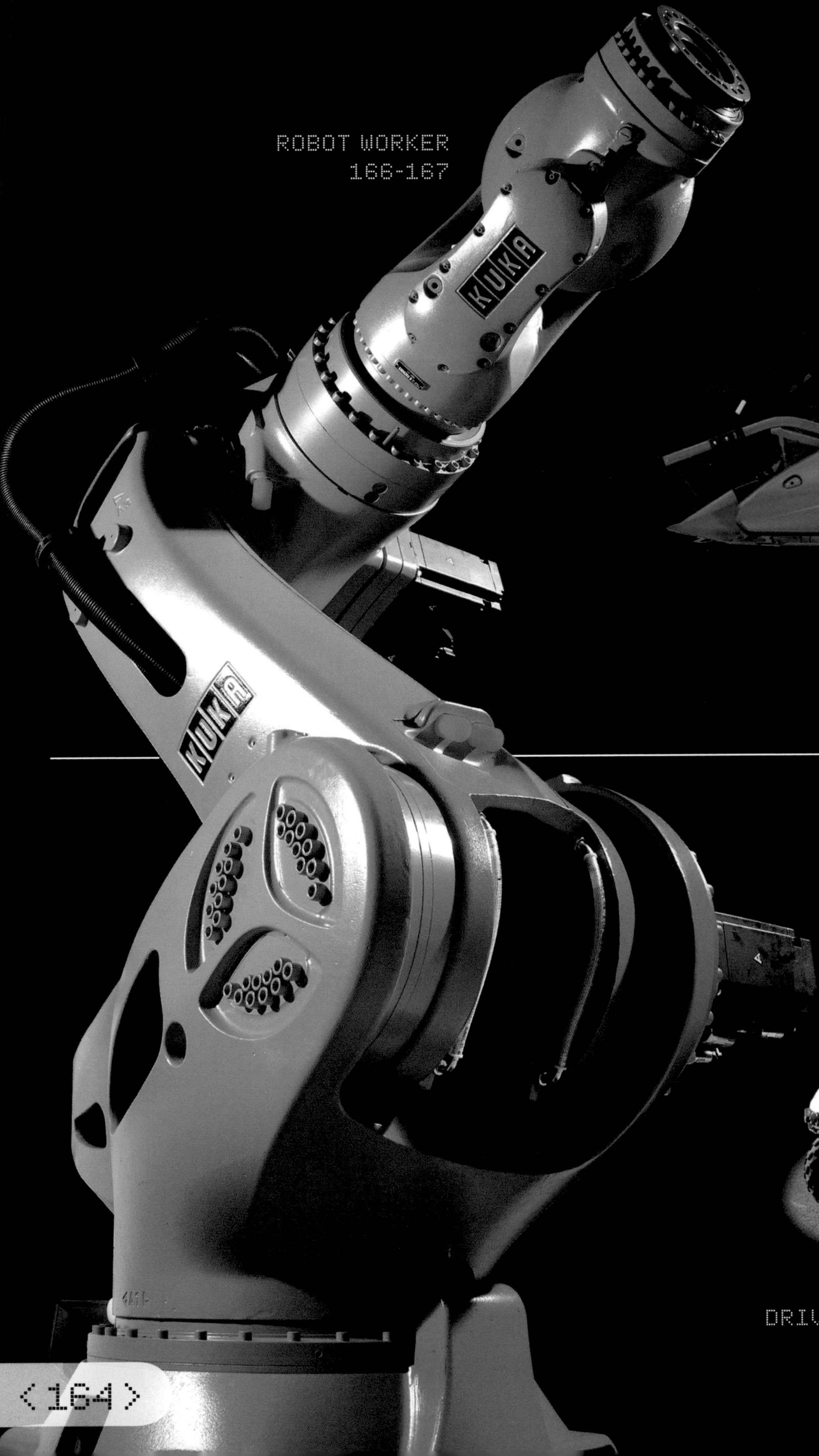

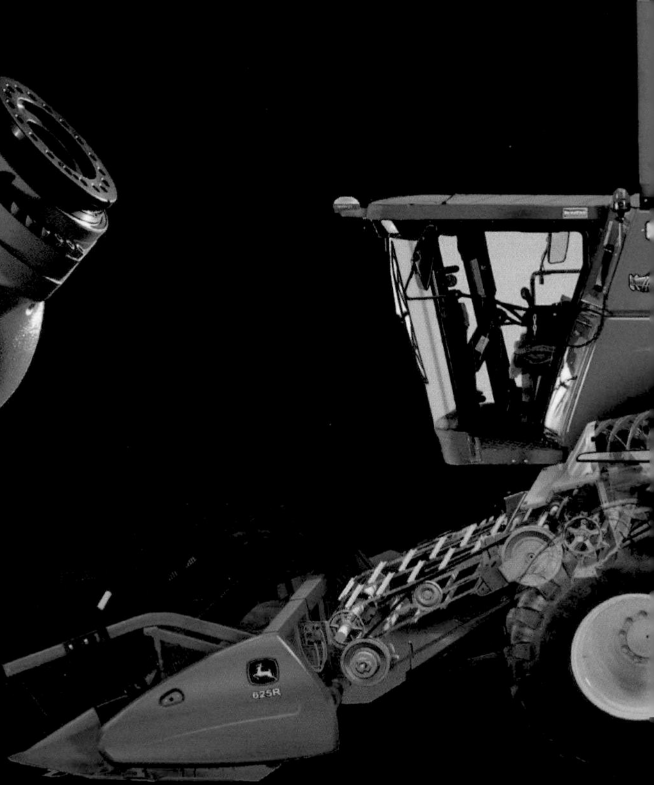

DRIVERLESS VEHICLE 168-169

< 164 >

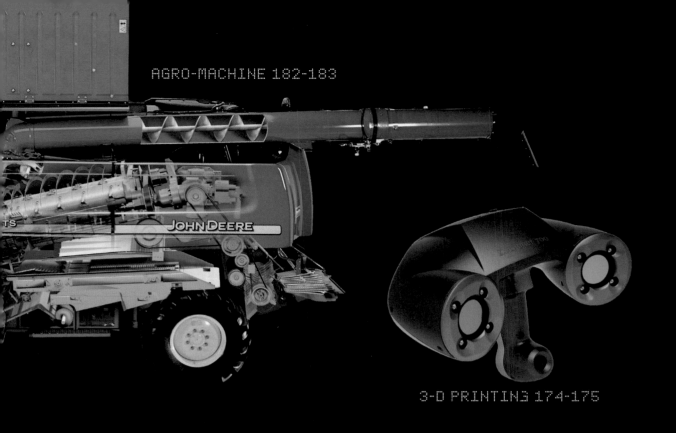

INDUSTRY

Clever gadgets and machines, such as MP3 players, computers, GPS devices, and digital cameras, are made by clever gadgets and machines! Today's factories work faster and smarter than ever before, using the latest "brainy" robots, self-adjusting assembly lines, and high-security controls. And year by year, the power stations that supply electricity to them—and us—become more intelligent, less wasteful, and safer.

ROBOT WORKER

They do the same job thousands of times every day, week after week, without getting tired, taking lunch breaks, or needing the restroom. All they ask for is an occasional few drops of oil, and a regular service to replace worn parts.

A typical assembly line for cars or trucks uses more than 500 robots of different shapes and sizes. They do the same job to the same accuracy, time after time. In this way, they have great advantages over human workers.

TEACHING ROBOTS

The robots' precision movements are first plotted on a computer.

Most factory robots are controlled by computers, which are programmed by a person who "teaches" the robot what to do. The instructions are in the form of electrical or radio signals that tell the robot exactly how to move using its electric motors and hydraulic pistons.

< 168 >

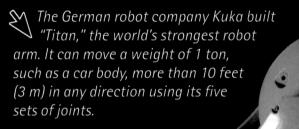
The German robot company Kuka built "Titan," the world's strongest robot arm. It can move a weight of 1 ton, such as a car body, more than 10 feet (3 m) in any direction using its five sets of joints.

Attachment socket

Hydraulic hose

Swivel joint

Different attachments at the end of a robot arm allow it to do different tasks, from lifting heavy loads to drilling holes exactly in the right place and to a precise depth.

ROBOT JOBS

Robots have taken over many routine factory tasks, from grinding and welding large pieces of metal to painting, drilling, nailing, screwing, and connecting delicate electronic circuits with pinpoint accuracy. The most adaptable robots are known as "six axis." They can move in six ways—forward and backward, side to side, up and down vertically, tilt up and down, lean to each side, and swivel or rotate left and right.

DRIVERLESS VEHICLES

Look, no hands—and no driver, either! Some driverless vehicles are experiments to test new technologies, such as sensors, computers that think for themselves, and car controls. Others are robots in factories, working night and day.

"David" took part in the 2004 World Challenge for robot cars, driving 150 miles (240 km) through the Mojave Desert.

Cameras

Laser range finders detect the distance of objects.

"Stanley" the Volkswagen Tuareg car has cameras, lasers, radar, and GPS. Its onboard computers decide which way to go and how fast.

< 168 >

LINKS < **88** SPORTS CAR **94** FUEL-CELL CAR **106** GPS

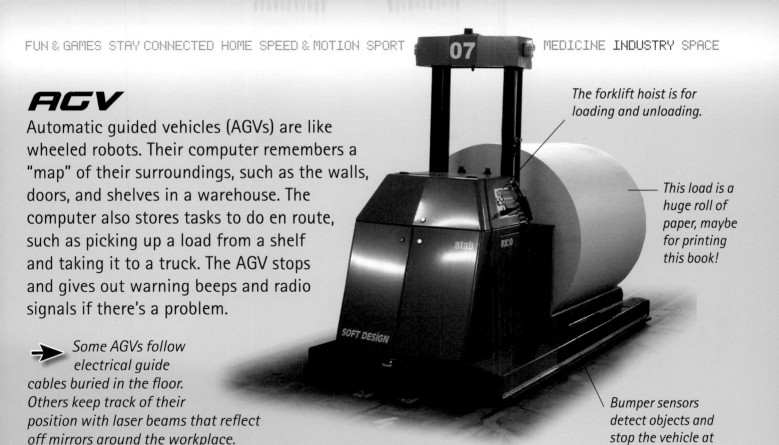

AGV

Automatic guided vehicles (AGVs) are like wheeled robots. Their computer remembers a "map" of their surroundings, such as the walls, doors, and shelves in a warehouse. The computer also stores tasks to do en route, such as picking up a load from a shelf and taking it to a truck. The AGV stops and gives out warning beeps and radio signals if there's a problem.

Some AGVs follow electrical guide cables buried in the floor. Others keep track of their position with laser beams that reflect off mirrors around the workplace.

The forklift hoist is for loading and unloading.

This load is a huge roll of paper, maybe for printing this book!

Bumper sensors detect objects and stop the vehicle at once if necessary.

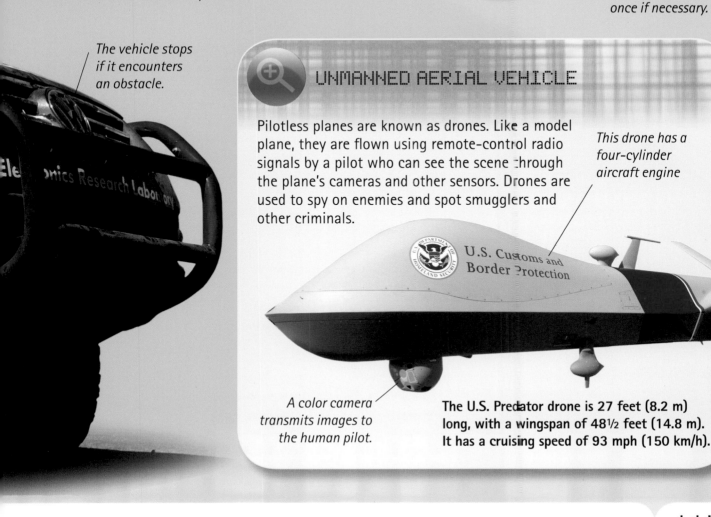

The vehicle stops if it encounters an obstacle.

UNMANNED AERIAL VEHICLE

Pilotless planes are known as drones. Like a model plane, they are flown using remote-control radio signals by a pilot who can see the scene through the plane's cameras and other sensors. Drones are used to spy on enemies and spot smugglers and other criminals.

This drone has a four-cylinder aircraft engine

U.S. Customs and Border Protection

A color camera transmits images to the human pilot.

The U.S. Predator drone is 27 feet (8.2 m) long, with a wingspan of 48½ feet (14.8 m). It has a cruising speed of 93 mph (150 km/h).

LASERS

A laser is a source of high-intensity radiation emitted from a solid, liquid, or gaseous medium. Many of the gadgets in this book, including barcode readers and fiber-optic cables, use lasers.

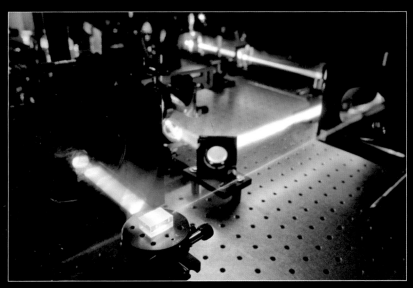

In scientific research, laser beams are split, angled, and bounced back on a large work area called a laser optical bench.

TYPES OF LASER

The first laser was invented in 1960. Today, there are dozens of types of laser. Most are named after their main active substance. Ruby lasers can be used to remove unwanted hair and tattoos. Carbon dioxide lasers are capable of emitting hundreds of kilowatts and can be very powerful. They are used for tasks ranging from cutting and welding heavy industrial parts to performing ultrafine surgery, using the laser to cut like a scalpel.

< 170 >
ESSENTIAL FOR > CDs · DVDs · retail · home security

HOW A LASER WORKS

A laser contains an "active medium," such as a crystal, glass, or gas, which receives pulses of energy in the form of electricity or light. The energy "pumps" this medium until its particles give off packages of light energy that bounce to and fro. When there are enough of them, they "break out" as laser light. Unlike ordinary light, a laser contains only one color. Its rays are in step with each other, so the beam stays thin.

1 *A ruby laser has an active medium of a ruby crystal rod, and a coiled quartz flash tube. The tube flashes bursts of light energy into the rod.*

2 *The rod's atoms absorb the flashes of light, which are packages of energy called photons, and become "excited."*

4 *When the photons reach the end of the crystal, they are reflected by a mirror. They bounce back along the crystal, making excited atoms emit identical photons as they go.*

3 *As a photon passes an "excited" atom, the atom emits its energy as another photon, moving in the same direction as the passing photon. The number of photons builds up, all traveling together.*

5 *The mirror at the end of the crystal is not perfectly reflective and does not bounce all the photons back into the crystal. One in 20 photons shoots out of the end, forming the laser beam.*

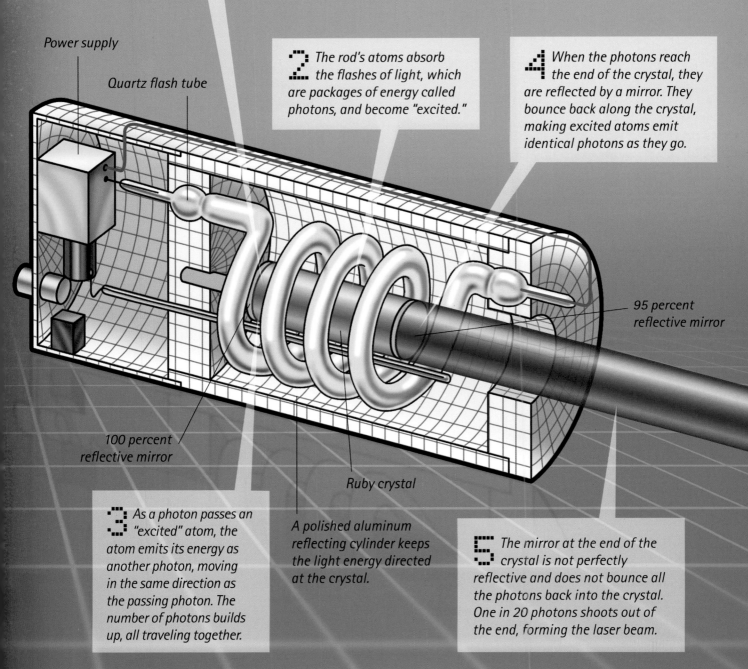

Power supply

Quartz flash tube

95 percent reflective mirror

100 percent reflective mirror

Ruby crystal

A polished aluminum reflecting cylinder keeps the light energy directed at the crystal.

INDUSTRIAL LASERS

Hundreds of different types of lasers are used in industry. The most powerful can melt metal and burn away solid rock. The most delicate are used to make microchips containing parts thousands of times smaller than this period.

Safety is vital when testing high-power lasers. Special spectacles, goggles, or visors prevent eye damage if the beam accidentally shines in the eye.

Testing a laser range finder (distance measurer) for a weapon.

CUT AND WELD

A computer controls the speed and direction of the cutting laser.

Carbon dioxide lasers produce light beams with so much energy that they can melt metal. The metal may be cut to make an accurate shape with smooth edges, or two metal parts side by side may have their edges melted so they flow together, creating a really strong joint called a weld.

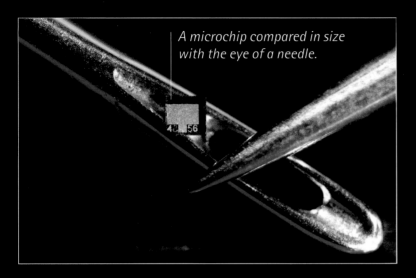

A microchip compared in size with the eye of a needle.

> Lasers can vaporize layers of silicon to "write" thousands of transistors and other electronic components onto a silicon chip small enough to pass through the eye of a needle.

LASER WATT

Lasers, like lightbulbs, have power measured in watts. The small lasers that read CDs are usually less than 5 mW (five-thousandths of a watt), while the laser that "burns" a new CD is 100–200 mW. Carbon dioxide lasers for cutting metal produce millions of watts of power. Some lasers are a continuous wave, producing a steady beam. Others are pulsed, where the beam flashes on and off, allowing more power.

> Barcode scanners detect whether the low-power laser they produce is reflected off a gap in the bar code.

> A laser level is used in surveying. It makes sure surfaces are flat before building commences.

ENGRAVING

Engraving lasers remove a thin layer from a surface by burning it into a vapor. The power is adjusted to control the depth of the layer, depending on the substance being engraved. A computer controls the laser's movement, enabling the laser to copy an original picture or writing.

A laser engraves a wooden plaque at high speed.

< 173 >

3-D PRINTER

The pages in this book are printed on a flat, two-dimensional surface. Three-dimensional, or 3-D, printing adds depth to produce a solid object. This brand-new technology can "print" all kinds of items, from plastic toys to complex working machines.

To copy a real object, its shape is captured by a two-camera laser scanner. Like our eyes, this sees the object from two slightly different angles, and stores it as 3-D information.

The scanner sends data back to a laptop.

SLICE BY SLICE

One type of 3-D printer uses layers of fine powder. The first layer of powder is spread, and the printer head sprays a shape onto it in a special ink. This colors the powder and also sticks its particles together. Loose powder is removed, a second layer of powder is added, and so forth, building up the object slice by slice.

After the final layer is completed, the object is lifted from the loose powder.

Model belts and pulleys are accurate and to scale.

Complicated shapes, such as this model of a car engine, can be built up layer by layer.

COMPUTER

When printing in three dimensions, the object's shape is stored in a computer's memory. The object could have been created from scratch using computer-aided design (CAD), or "scanned" from an existing object. The shape can be made smaller or larger, stretched or squeezed, before the information is fed into the 3-D printer to make a perfect replica.

As a two-camera laser scanner moves over an object, it feeds information into a laptop computer. The dots help the computer recognize what it has already seen as the scanner adds new areas.

RAPID PROTOTYPES

A hub cap is built up in layers of plastic powder.

Prototypes are trial versions of a new object. They are often made by hand using expensive tools and materials. In rapid prototyping, an object is designed on a computer and then made by a 3-D printer in a few hours.

SECURI-TECH

Not so long ago, a document with your photograph was the only identification you needed at an airport or to enter a high-security zone. Today, sophisticated technology is used to make sure you are who you say you are, and that no one's carrying a weapon.

Normal X-rays go straight through clothes and soft body parts. Backscatter X-rays, shown here, bounce back off different materials, depending on the distance they travel. They can even "see" under clothes.

A hidden weapon is revealed.

BIOMETRIC CHIPS

"Biometric" means "measuring life." Measurements are taken of body parts, such as the eyes, face, and fingerprints, and are stored on a microchip in a smart card or biometric passport. At a security check, a special camera can compare the measurements of a person with those on the chip in the passport.

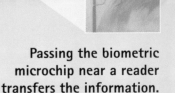

Passing the biometric microchip near a reader transfers the information.

The microchip is sealed into the passport cover.

IRIS SCANNING

The iris is the colored part of the eye. No two eyes, even of the same person, have the same iris pattern of tiny colored lines and streaks. This makes the iris an excellent guide to a person's identity. In iris scanning, a camera takes a detailed picture of the iris, which is scanned by computer and converted into digital codes. Compared to fingerprints, the iris is less likely to cause a false match and is almost impossible to fake.

 A picture of the iris is taken using infrared light, which can reveal more detail than normal light. It is quick and safe and works fine with glasses or contact lenses.

The iris is read by a scanner and matched to personal details, such as your name.

FINGERPRINT SCANNING

No two people have the same fingerprints— the patterns of ridges and swirls on fingertip skin. A fingertip placed on a glass sheet can be scanned and its unique pattern stored. At the next identification check, the new scan is compared with the stored information to make sure it is the same person.

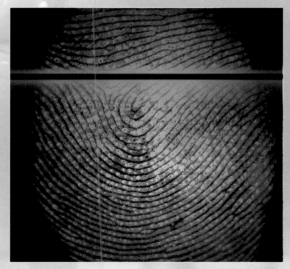

A computer converts the unique patterns on a fingerprint into digital code.

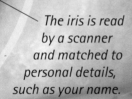 *In facial recognition, a computer measures features, such as distance between the eyes, nose length, and ear position, and stores this information. Any face picture can then be compared for a match. It's not as accurate as iris or fingerprint scans.*

⟩ **180** IDENTI-ME **216** GLOSSARY: BIOMETRIC

NANOTECH

"Nano" is not just small, or even microscopic—it's tinier than that. Nanotechnology builds objects and machines at the scale of individual bits of matter called atoms, by joining them together to form molecules.

NANOSCALE

One nanometer (nm) is a billionth of a meter. (1 meter = approx 3 feet.) One nm is about a million times smaller than the dot on this "i." "Nanoman" (left), built by Birmingham University researchers from single carbon atoms, is 400 nm tall. If 10,000 stood on each other's heads, they would be as tall as this "I."

300 nm (0.00003 mm)

The "nanocar" is made from carbon atoms. It has an H-shaped framework and four wheels made of nanoballs. If it's heated up to 392°F on a pure gold surface, it slides along.

The parts of the nanocar are made from individual atoms.

A typical carbon atom is about 0.25 nm, or one-quarter of a nanometer across.

EVERYDAY USES

Most industrial processes are "top down." They start big and get smaller. For example, a lump of metal is cut, ground down, and drilled into a precise shape. This uses large amounts of energy and produces much waste. One idea behind nanotechnology is to build from the "bottom up." Atoms and molecules are joined together chemically to make a precisely shaped object, wasting less energy and materials.

 Everyday items made using nanotech include tennis balls that keep their bounce longer, sunscreens that protect the skin better, and clothing fibers that are easier to clean.

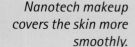

Nanotech makeup covers the skin more smoothly.

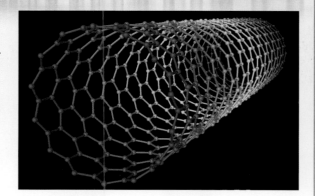

 This image depicts how huge a human hair would be, shown against a city for scale, if enlarged by the amount a real man is larger than the nanoman shown opposite.

NANOTUBES

Carbon is very useful in nanotechnology. Its atoms can join together in different patterns, such as squares and hexagons. Many linked hexagons can form a nanotube. Pentagons and hexagons can be linked to form a nanoball that can be used in nanomachines.

Carbon nanotubes are very light yet incredibly strong.

IDENTI-ME

There are billions of bar codes and RFID tags in the world. Most people use them every day without realizing it. "RFID" stands for "radio frequency identification device." It's an electronic gadget that transmits radio waves about its identity.

Most products (including this book) carry bar codes. These barcode lines are scanned by a laser in order to identify the product.

BARCODES

Barcodes are found on all kinds of products and packaging. They consist of dark bars against a white background. The width and spacing of each bar represents a number. When the barcode is scanned by a laser or camera, it is fed into a computer, which converts it into numbers to identify the product.

A pen scanner checks the barcode label on a blood sample tube.

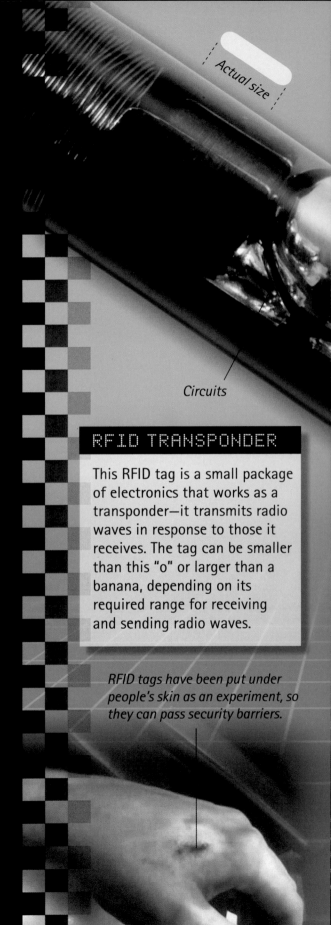

Actual size

Circuits

RFID TRANSPONDER

This RFID tag is a small package of electronics that works as a transponder—it transmits radio waves in response to those it receives. The tag can be smaller than this "o" or larger than a banana, depending on its required range for receiving and sending radio waves.

RFID tags have been put under people's skin as an experiment, so they can pass security barriers.

ESSENTIAL FOR > retail · security · factory production

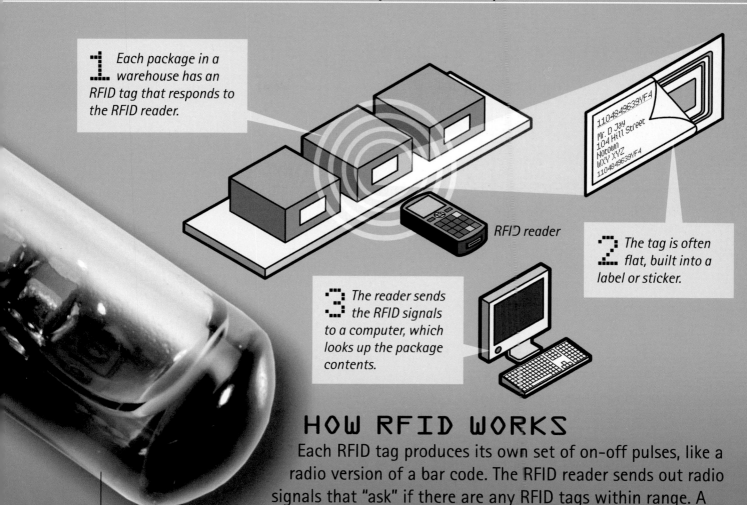

1. *Each package in a warehouse has an RFID tag that responds to the RFID reader.*

RFID reader

2. *The tag is often flat, built into a label or sticker.*

3. *The reader sends the RFID signals to a computer, which looks up the package contents.*

110 4849639YF4
Mr. D Jay
104 Hill Street
Notown
WXY XYZ
110 4849639YF4

Antenna (aerial) to send and receive radio waves.

HOW RFID WORKS

Each RFID tag produces its own set of on-off pulses, like a radio version of a bar code. The RFID reader sends out radio signals that "ask" if there are any RFID tags within range. A tag responds by sending out a unique code, with information about its product. An RFID tag doesn't have batteries. Its radio signals are powered by the signals it receives from the reader.

RFID NETWORK

Many types of smart cards, such as the Oyster cards used on underground trains and buses in London, England, use RFID tags. Each time the card is placed on a reader, the reader questions the tag and the tag responds, all in a split second. The information goes to a central computer, which can update the card-holder's account by deducting or adding money.

An Oyster card used on London public transport.

oyster™

AMAZING FACT > The first product to have a barcode scanned was a package of Wrigley's gum.

< 181 >

AGRO-MACHINE

Combine harvesters have been around for about 180 years. Today, onboard computer technology allows the latest agro machines to harvest vast areas of farmland faster and more efficiently than ever before.

The combine harvester cuts the crop, threshes it by shaking the grain from the stalks and other unwanted bits, and stores the grain in a tank until it's loaded into a trailer.

TOTAL CONTROL

GPS receiver

Soundproofed, air-conditioned cab

This touch screen updates every second.

A touch screen displays information on the combine, from engine temperature and fuel level to the weight of grain onboard. The GPS screens display maps of the field showing how much is left to harvest.

The feeder conveyor carries the crop into the machine.

GPS

Satellite photographs of a farm's fields show the crops as they ripen. The farmer uses the photographs to decide which areas to harvest on which days. The combine's onboard GPS (satellite navigation) system pinpoints the combine's position and uses the coordinates from the photographs to work out where to start. The combine can even drive itself there.

The harvester's radio aerials and GPS receiver may need adjusting for the best signals, depending on the direction of the crop rows being harvested.

This corkscrew moves grain along the unloading tube.

The unloading tube pours grain into a trailer or truck.

A turbocharged diesel engine powers all the machinery.

JOHN DEERE

A sensor in the grain tank tracks the amount of grain inside and radios this to a computer. The computer then works out if the year is a good one for that field.

Raking device

WIND TURBINE

Giant turbines in wind farms are a common feature of today's landscape. Wind turbines turn the force of the wind into green electricity—a source that doesn't burn polluting fossil fuels. A single turbine can generate enough electricity to power 1,000 homes.

INSIDE THE POD

Engineers clean and adjust the machinery, such as the gears and brake, inside the pod.

Most of the time a wind turbine works automatically. Its radio link to a local control station shows wind strength, how much electricity is being made, and whether the equipment is working properly. An engineer visits regularly, climbing a spiral staircase in the tower to check and maintain the machinery.

Huge bearings inside the hub make the shaft turn smoothly.

The most common wind turbines have huge blades or rotors on a spinning hub. This is attached to a pod on top of a tall tower or pylon. The pod and blades turn to face the wind.

The turbine pylon is built from sections of steel tubing. The blades are then lifted up one by one, using a huge mobile crane, and bolted to the main shaft.

Sensors on the pod monitor wind speed and direction.

The rotor blades on the largest wind turbines are more than 200 feet (60 m) long.

ROTORS

The rotor blades can twist on the shaft to change the angle at which they face the wind and to control their spin speed. In high winds, they are angled almost edge on so that they do not spin too fast and topple the whole turbine. In light winds, they twist so that the flat surface faces the wind to catch as much wind energy as possible.

An engineer checks the radio and weather-recording equipment.

This aerial provides the radio link.

Offshore wind farms are built on concrete foundations in shallow waters. Electricity comes ashore through buried cables. Offshore farms are less of an "eyesore," but ships must be careful.

WIND FARMS

Several wind turbines together are called a wind farm. Sites are chosen for the presence of consistent winds throughout the year. Wind provides free, sustainable—meaning it won't run out—pollution-free, long-term energy. Because the wind cannot be guaranteed, however, we also need other ways of making electricity. Some people also complain about the wind turbines spoiling the view and about the loud whooshing noises that they make.

LINKS ‹ **62** ECO HOME **64** SOLAR CELL **186** POWER STATION **216** GLOSSARY: GENERATOR ›

POWER STATION

Electricity is the world's favorite form of energy. Flick a switch and it powers endless gadgets. Most electricity comes from burning fossil fuels, which make polluting fumes and speed up global warming. Making electricity from cleaner sources, and using it in smarter ways, can help reduce these problems.

 Lights blaze all night in big cities, such as London in England, shown here in a satellite picture. Electricity use is high, 24 hours a day.

TYPES OF POWER STATION

Worldwide, more than two-thirds of electricity comes from burning coal, gas, oil, and other fossil fuels. About one-seventh comes from nuclear power. A similar amount comes from hydropower, where electricity is generated by water flowing past turbines, making them spin and turn generators.

This Danish power station makes electricity from natural gas.

In a modern power station control room, operators can see at a glance what's happening in the boilers, steam pipes, turbines, and generators.

 LINKS ‹ **62** ECO HOME **184** WIND TURBINE

THE GRID

All power stations feed their electricity into a huge network known as the grid. The grid controllers check how much electricity is being used and what the demand is likely to be, according to the time of day, the weather, and popular TV events, such as the Superbowl. They feed back this information to the power stations, telling them to reduce or expand their output.

Power station operators monitor factors, such as turbine speed and pressure.

The display provides a virtual "map" of the power station.

STEAM TURBINES

The steam turbines are checked carefully when the power station is taken "off line."

In most power stations, burning fuel boils water into high-pressure steam. This blasts past the angled blades of a turbine to make it spin. The turbine is joined to a generator and spins its coils of wire in a strong magnetic field, which produces electricity.

FUSION REACTOR

Sometime this century, nuclear fusion reactors could be making electricity using the same process that powers the sun. Nuclear fusion happens when small atoms of hydrogen are forced together, releasing tremendous energy and very little waste.

 STAR POWER

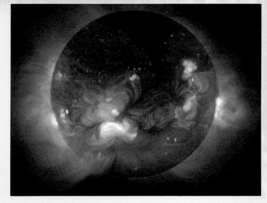

Stars burn by fusion reactions.

The sun and other stars make incredible amounts of heat and other energy by natural fusion power. Colossal pressures and temperatures at the sun's core create trillions of reactions each second, as fused hydrogen atoms release energy and create helium.

➡ *JET, the Joint European Torus, near Oxford, is the largest nuclear fusion test reactor ever built. Completed in 1983, it only reaches full power for a few seconds at a time.*

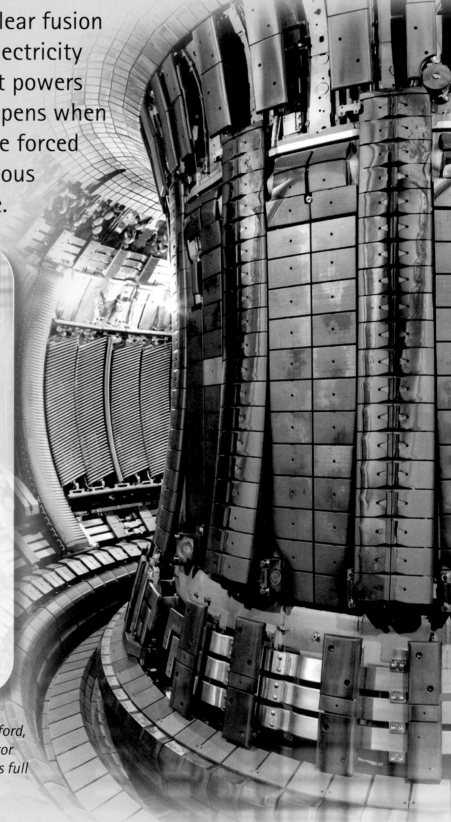

This view of the inner JET chamber tokamak is superimposed with an image of the plasma taken by an infrared spectrum camera.

Sections of the fusion chamber join together to form a doughnut shape called a torus.

 ## MAKING PLASMA

To make fusion happen, fuel is heated to 1.8 billion degrees Fahrenheit—over six times hotter than the center of the sun. When fuel is this hot, it turns into a substance called plasma. Its particles fuse and release their energy as more heat, which is the useful part of the reaction.

The JET chamber is about 6½ feet (2 m) high.

INSIDE

The plasma inside the ring-shaped fusion chamber is so hot that it would instantly vaporize any substance, so it is kept away from the inner walls by magnetic forces. These are created by massively powerful electromagnets sited around the chamber. The plasma swirls around but never touches the shiny inner walls of the JET chamber. The machine that fuses the atoms within the chamber is called a tokamak.

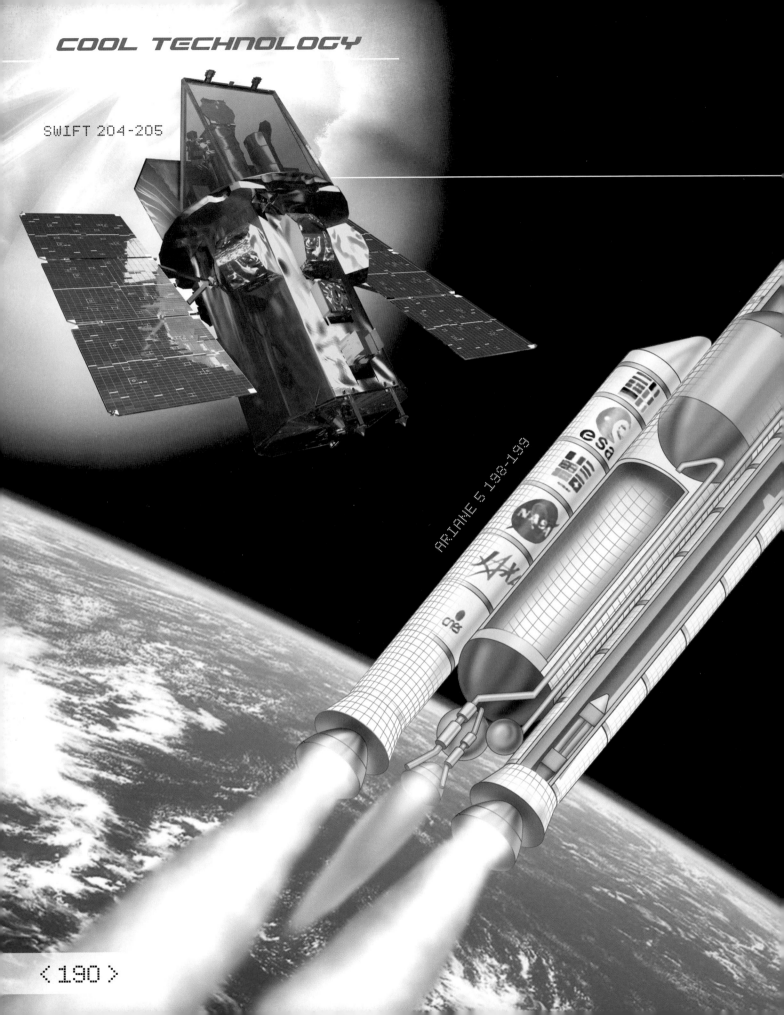

SWIFT 204-205

ARIANE 5 198-199

In 1957, *Sputnik 1*, a Russian satellite, became the first craft ever launched into space. In 1969, the first humans reached the Moon on the USA's *Apollo 11*. Today, spacecraft have traveled to the edges of our solar system, probes trundle about on Mars searching for alien microbes in the soil, satellites chase comets and return with samples of stardust, and shuttles take astronauts to work on the International Space Station.

CANADARM 202-203

PHOENIX MARS LANDER 208-209

VLT

The Very Large Telescope in Chile, South America, is formed from seven separate telescopes designed to work together to produce one image. This incredibly powerful telescope can see deep into space.

Each VLT telescope has a main mirror 27 feet (8.2 m) across. To correct distortions, levers attached to electric motors bend the mirror by tiny amounts.

The four main VLT telescopes have their own observatory buildings. Three smaller telescopes, each with a mirror 6 feet (1.8 m) across, can be moved to help "fill in" the scene.

The telescopes all align to look at one object.

All four views equal one telescope 52 feet (16 m) across.

VLT MIRRORS

The VLT telescopes are reflectors—they use enormous, curved mirrors to collect light from space and bounce it into various cameras. Because the mirrors degrade over time, they are resurfaced every year. The VLT collects the light from separate telescopes and re-combines it to give a much more detailed view than one telescope acting alone. This is known as interferometry.

The VLT's mirrors are accurate to a millionth of a yard.

The VLT has captured many distant objects in astonishing detail. This image of spiral galaxy NGC 3190, which is 80 million light years away, was taken with a 14-minute exposure.

VLT SITE

The VLT is located at the Paranal Observatory, 8530 feet (2,600 m) above sea level in the Atacama Desert of Chile. Here the skies are clear for about 350 nights a year. There is no light or air pollution to reduce the performance of the telescopes, and no water vapor in the high, dry air to blur and distort the view into space—a problem known as atmospheric distortion.

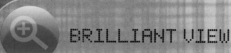

BRILLIANT VIEW

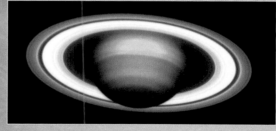

Saturn photographed in infrared by the VLT.

The VLT can pick out objects that other telescopes do not see, or can provide a much closer view. In addition to the planets of our solar system, the VLT has photographed planets that go around other stars—planets that may harbor life.

> 210 CASSINI–HUYGENS 216 GLOSSARY: INTERFEROMETRY

< 193 >

MISSION CONTROL

Space missions are managed by a mission control center. There, flight controllers monitor the launch and course of a craft using radio signals and the most up-to-date computer technology. The world's largest mission controller is NASA.

NASA's Johnson Space Center is busy 24 hours every day, checking launch systems, craft positions and functions, and the condition of astronauts in space.

JOHNSON SPACE CENTER

A space shuttle being transported.

The JSC near Houston, Texas, is the U.S. center for manned missions (not unmanned probes). It has more than 100 buildings, and 3,000 staff, including 100 astronauts, work there. The center trains astronauts in everything from basic science to space shuttle activities.

Touch-sensitive screens

MISSION EXPERTS

Different experts deal with different parts of a space mission. Some monitor the flight path and fuel levels and engines of a rocket. Payload specialists deal with the rocket's cargo, such as a satellite or probe. Life support specialists make sure the astronauts are healthy and well equipped. All the information passes up to space and back down to Earth via radio signals.

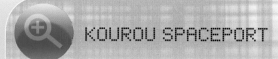

KOUROU SPACEPORT

An ESA rocket blasting off.

The main launchpad for the European Space Agency (ESA) is at Kourou in French Guiana on the northern coast of South America. It is 310 miles (500 km) from the equator, where the planet's spin is fastest. This gives rockets blasting off a good forward speed for orbit. If there's a problem, the rocket lands in the sea.

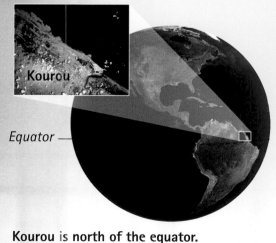

Kourou

Equator

Kourou is north of the equator.

SPACE SHUTTLE

NASA's space shuttle lifts off with the aid of massive booster rockets. It can carry eight crew and 32 tons (29 tonnes) of cargo into orbit, where smaller rockets maneuver it into position. The shuttle glides back to Earth and lands on a runway.

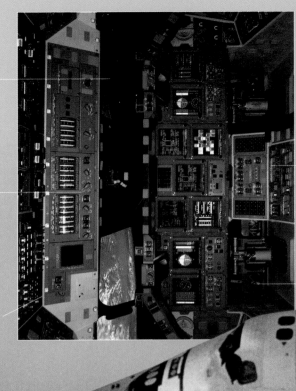

Glass window

Communications array

Navigation controls

System controls

Thruster control

The space shuttle's flight deck resembles that of a jet plane. Many of the controls and displays have a second set in case one fails.

Endeavour

External tank containing liquid fuel

Solid rocket booster

ARIANE

Ariane 5 launching.

Europe's main launchers are Ariane rockets. *Ariane 5* is 194 feet (59 m) high and weighs 856 tons (777 tonnes) fully fueled. Two boosters help during the first two minutes of flight, when its fuel load is heaviest and Earth's gravity is strongest. The boosters detach at 41 miles (66 km) high and parachute into the sea. They are collected and reused in the next mission.

Most rockets are ELVs, or expendable launch vehicles—they cannot be used again. All four parts of the space shuttle, including the planelike orbiter, can be reused. The massive fuel tanks are jettisoned but then recovered from the sea.

Payload doors
(where cargo is loaded)

Engines

United States

The nose casing and boosters fall away in orbit.

PAYLOADS

A payload is what a rocket carries into space. It could be a satellite to orbit Earth, a probe that heads into deep space, a crew of astronauts or parts for a space station. From 2015, U.S. lunar missions will use different vehicles to transport crew and cargo. The heavy cargo launch vehicle (shown right), powered by five shuttle engines and two boosters, will lift more than 110 tons 1(00 tonnes).

ROCKET ENGINE

All space launch vehicles are powered by rockets. Rocket engines burn fuel, and burning uses up oxygen. There's no oxygen in space, so rockets need to take their own oxygen with them as well as fuel.

The nozzle is the cone-shape part under the engine.

REACTION

A basic law of science says that for every action there's an opposite reaction. When a cannon ball shoots out, the cannon is pushed backward. As a rocket engine burns fuel, hot gases roar downward out of the nozzles at the bottom. This downward force is the action. The reaction force pushes the engine upward, carrying the rocket with it.

Burning fuel from a rocket engine creates huge amounts of smoke.

SOYUZ

Russia's main launcher is the Soyuz. The central engine has four huge nozzles surrounded by four boosters. The smaller nozzles can be controlled by a computer to make the rocket fly in the right direction.

< 198 > ESSENTIAL FOR > launch vehicles · space shuttle orbiter · space probes

HOW ROCKETS WORK

A rocket (such as the *Ariane 5*) burns fuel to make a blast of hot gases, like a continuous explosion, that carry it upward. Rocket fuels can be solid, liquid, or gas. Hydrogen, for example, is a fuel kept in a very cold liquid form. The oxygen for burning comes from an oxidizer, which is often liquid oxygen. The fuel and oxidizer together are known as propellants.

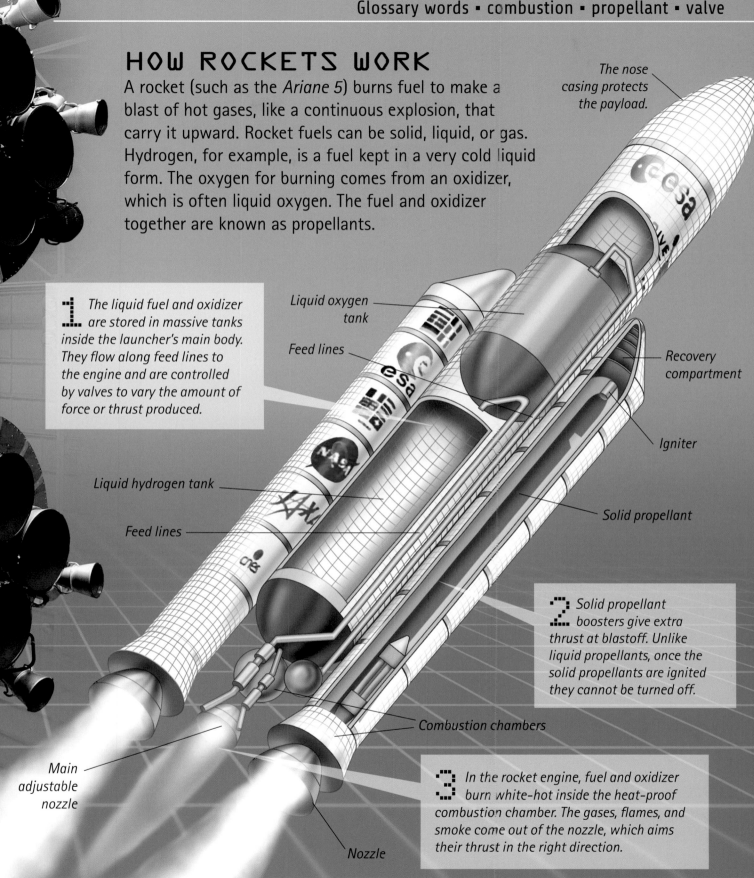

The nose casing protects the payload.

1 *The liquid fuel and oxidizer are stored in massive tanks inside the launcher's main body. They flow along feed lines to the engine and are controlled by valves to vary the amount of force or thrust produced.*

Liquid oxygen tank

Feed lines

Recovery compartment

Igniter

Liquid hydrogen tank

Feed lines

Solid propellant

2 *Solid propellant boosters give extra thrust at blastoff. Unlike liquid propellants, once the solid propellants are ignited they cannot be turned off.*

Combustion chambers

Main adjustable nozzle

3 *In the rocket engine, fuel and oxidizer burn white-hot inside the heat-proof combustion chamber. The gases, flames, and smoke come out of the nozzle, which aims their thrust in the right direction.*

Nozzle

AMAZING FACT > The *Ariane 5* (above) can carry a 6.6-ton (6-tonne) payload into orbit.

DAY TRIPS TO SPACE

In the future, it may be possible to leave Earth not by rocket, but by plane—or even by elevator. A space plane can take off and return from a runway. A space elevator would simply lift you up into orbit.

In 2004, SpaceShipOne became the first private craft to be launched into space.

Pilot's cockpit

328KF

SpaceShipOne

SCALED COMPOSITES

Upper rudder steers craft while in atmosphere.

SPACESHIPTWO

The Virgin Galactic project aims to build an improved version of SpaceShipOne known as SpaceShipTwo. It will have a single-rocket engine, a top speed of 2,485 miles (4,000 km) per hour, large porthole windows, and eight seats. Passengers will be weightless for six minutes as the craft journeys beyond the 62-mile (100-km) limit that marks the start of space.

Inside, SpaceShipTwo is the same width as a small business jet plane.

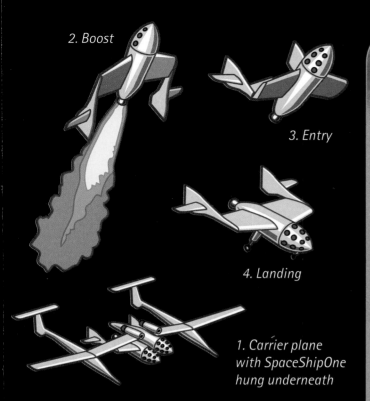

2. Boost

3. Entry

4. Landing

1. Carrier plane
with SpaceShipOne
hung underneath

SpaceShipOne is taken 10 miles (16 km)
up by a carrier plane. It changes its wing
positions as it boosts into space, reenters the
atmosphere, and lands on a runway.

SPACE TOURISTS

Both SpaceShipOne and SpaceShipTwo
are suborbital craft, which means that
they zoom up into space and straight
back down, rather than orbit Earth. A
space plane can take off from a runway
like an ordinary plane, fly into space, and
return for a smooth landing, all in a day.
The main attraction of space tourism is
to experience weightlessness and
the intense thrill of gazing upon
Earth from space.

SPACE ELEVATOR

A space elevator could do away with rockets
altogether. A long cable would extend from Earth's
surface far into space. Climber devices would crawl
up the cable, taking loads, such as satellites, space
probes, and parts for space stations, to be released at
different heights.

The climber would grip the
cable with wheels or claws.

The elevator cable would be
22,230 miles (35,780 km)
long (almost three times
the width of Earth). At
the end, a counterweight
satellite orbits Earth
once every 24 hours,
going directly above
the anchor station.

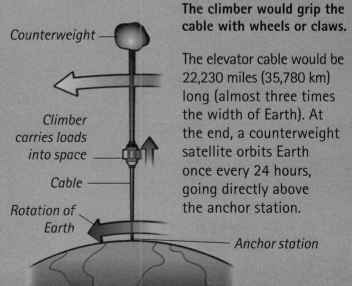

Counterweight

Climber
carries loads
into space

Cable

Rotation of
Earth

Anchor station

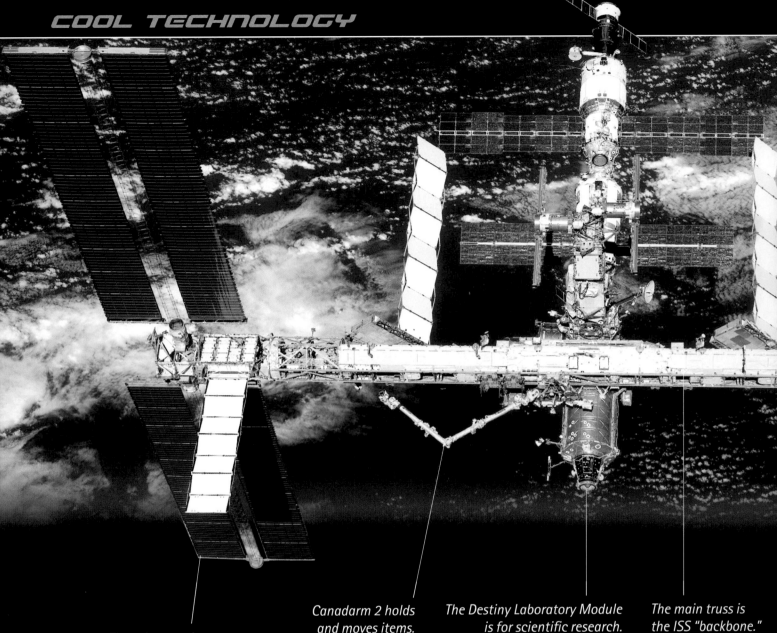

Canadarm 2 holds
and moves items.

The Destiny Laboratory Module
is for scientific research.

The main truss is
the ISS "backbone."

The solar panels turn
sunlight into electricity.

The ISS moves at
almost 26 feet (8 m)
per second, orbiting
Earth nearly 16 times
each day. It has several
modules for living,
working, and observing.
Visiting spacecraft make
airtight attachments to
it at the docking ports.

INTERNATIONAL SPACE STATION

Since 1998, the International Space Station (ISS) has gradually been built from parts taken up by space shuttles and Russian launchers. It should be complete by 2011. It can sometimes be seen from Earth as a fast-moving dot in the night sky.

LINKS ‹ 194 MISSION CONTROL 196 SPACE SHUTTLE

LIFE SUPPORT

The life support technology in the ISS is vital for survival. Electric heaters provide warmth. The air is filtered and recycled, with vital oxygen added by an Elektron machine, which splits molecules of water into hydrogen and oxygen atoms. All the water, including washing water and urine, must be recycled and purified.

EFFECTS OF ZERO GRAVITY

Because it is in orbit, the ISS is constantly "falling" in a circle. Inside, the ISS astronauts don't notice how fast they are going but do notice that the ground doesn't push up against their feet. Everything is weightless and floats about if not secured to something.

Astronauts gather in the main module for a "family photo."

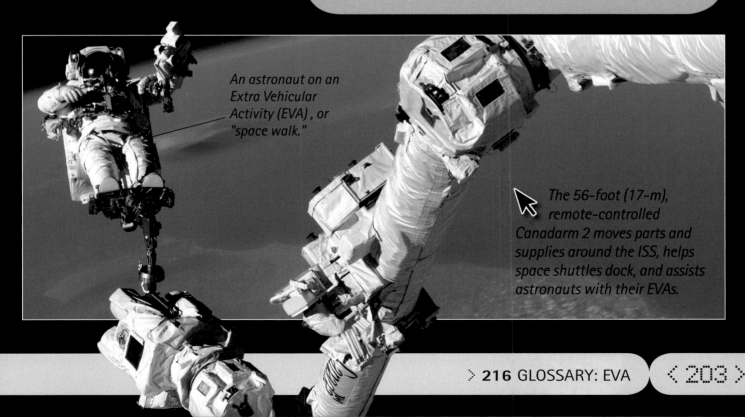

An astronaut on an Extra Vehicular Activity (EVA), or "space walk."

The 56-foot (17-m), remote-controlled Canadarm 2 moves parts and supplies around the ISS, helps space shuttles dock, and assists astronauts with their EVAs.

SATELLITES

Artificial satellites are devices designed to orbit Earth, the Sun, the Moon, or another planet. They are used for communication or to transmit scientific data back to Earth. Satellites are launched into orbit by rockets.

WHAT SWIFT DOES

To detect gamma rays, Swift is fitted with a "mask" made of 52,000 tiny lead plates.

Swift was launched in 2004 to study the mysterious gamma-ray bursts (GRBs) coming from deep space. Since then it has observed about two per week. GRBs are the most powerful explosions in the universe. They are thought to be caused by the collapse of massive stars or by collisions between dense stellar bodies millions or billions of light years away.

Swift is 20 feet (6 m) long, weighs 1.5 tons, and orbits Earth 375 miles (600 km) high every 90 minutes. It is solar-powered.

X-ray and ultraviolet telescopes.

Lead mask

Solar panels turn sunlight into electricity.

Launched in 2006, the two Stereos take images at the same time from millions of miles apart. Computers turn them into three-dimensional pictures that give more information than two-dimensional images.

Each Stereo is about 21 feet (6.5 m) wide, including the solar panels.

WHAT STEREO DOES

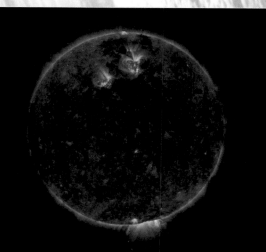

Seen here in ultraviolet light, the Sun's surface seethes with flares and storms.

Stereo is not one satellite but two. They orbit the Sun, with Stereo A more than 620,000 miles (100,000,000 km) ahead of the orbiting Earth, and Stereo B a similar distance behind. They take pictures and record activity on the Sun's surface, and watch for the ejection particles that form the "solar wind." This gives warning of magnetic storms from the Sun that can cause power blackouts on Earth.

RETURN MISSIONS

Some probes have traveled deep into space to bring back rocks, dust, and other samples from asteroids and comets. One day, probes may return with samples from other planets.

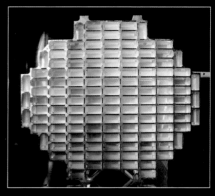

 Stardust's particle collector is about the size of a tennis racket. It is made from blocks of aerogel, a soft, spongy substance almost as light as air.

STARDUST

The Stardust probe collected about one million tiny particles, mainly from Comet Wild 2 and from open space. The largest specks were the size of this period. The particles were tested by scientists around the world, and were found to contain many types of crystals and mineral substances, but no traces of the water essential for life.

A comet particle impact caught in aerogel.

The particle collector folded out of the open sample container.

The dish aerial (antenna) sent and received radio signals.

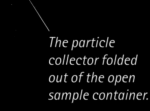 *After a 1.9-billion-mile (3-billion-km) trip to Comet Wild 2 to collect dust, Stardust returned to Earth orbit in 2006. It dropped its sample capsule, and headed back into deep space.*

DEEP IMPACT

In 2005, spacecraft Deep Impact released a washing-machine-size device with a camera attached toward nearby Comet Tempel. The camera took pictures, which it radioed back to Deep Impact. This then sent the pictures to Earth along with its own images. The aim was to find out what a comet's head (nucleus) is made of—fine dust, frozen gases, and a lot of empty space.

Deep Impact releases its probe, called an impactor.

HAYABUSA

Hayabusa is a Japanese unmanned mission to bring back space samples. Launched in 2003, it ran into a number of problems but eventually reached its destination, asteroid Itokawa, in 2005. Despite losing two of its four engines and a tiny, robotic camera spacecraft, it managed to collect some samples and is due to return to Earth in 2010.

Hayabusa's problems included power cuts, broken wheels, and leaky thrusters. But it still landed on an asteroid 186 million miles (300 million km) from Earth.

Hayabusa's sensor provides navigational data to guide its landing.

PHOENIX MARS LANDER

Mars has been visited by more spacecraft than any other planet, but more than half have disappeared or crash-landed. NASA's Phoenix, which reached the Red Planet in May 2008, is the latest to make the voyage.

The main deck of Phoenix is 5 feet (1.5 m) across.

Phoenix blasted off before dawn on August 4, 2007, from Cape Canaveral, Florida, on top of a Delta 2 rocket. It is the 40th mission to Mars.

Phoenix is a "soft lander," using jets of gas to settle slowly onto the Martian surface. It carries a special DVD full of Mars photographs and messages that might be viewed by future astronauts—or aliens.

The legs have springs to absorb the landing bump.

 SOLAR PANELS

Two octagonal solar panel "wings" will provide the Phoenix with power. The onset of winter in the far north of Mars will mark the end of the mission since there will be no sunlight for the panels to recharge the lander's batteries. As the atmosphere cools, frost will cover the region and bury the lander in ice.

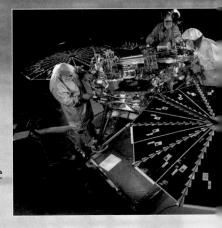

LOOKING FOR LIFE

Phoenix aims to look for signs of water on Mars, and even possible life—not little green men, but microscopic blobs similar to microbes on Earth. They might not be alive now, but deep frozen and preserved from a time when Mars was warmer and had liquid water. Phoenix is the first craft designed to explore a polar region of Mars, near the North Pole at the top of the planet. There may be soil there under the frozen surface.

MARS SCIENCE LAB

The cameras are mounted on a tall mast.

Since 2004, two small rovers, Spirit and Opportunity, have trundled around on Mars. In 2010, a much bigger rover is due. The Mars Science Lab will collect rocks and soil for tests to see if there are any traces of water or life forms.

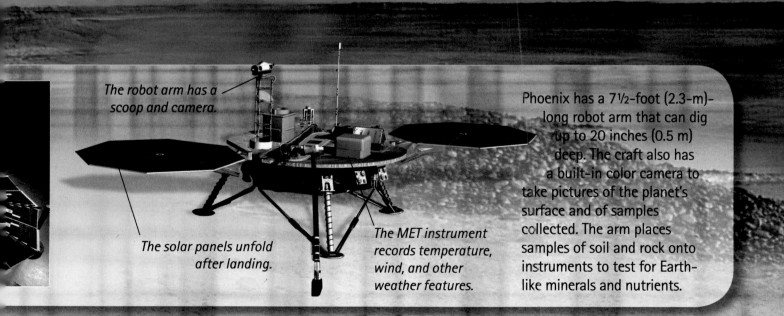

The robot arm has a scoop and camera.

The solar panels unfold after landing.

The MET instrument records temperature, wind, and other weather features.

Phoenix has a 7½-foot (2.3-m)-long robot arm that can dig up to 20 inches (0.5 m) deep. The craft also has a built-in color camera to take pictures of the planet's surface and of samples collected. The arm places samples of soil and rock onto instruments to test for Earth-like minerals and nutrients.

CASSINI-HUYGENS

In October 1997, the probe Cassini–Huygens was launched. Timing was vital. There was a brief "launch window" for the shortest journey, when Earth and the target planet, Saturn, were at their nearest. Otherwise, the journey would have taken 70 years—not 7.

DEEP-SPACE PROBE

In 2004, after almost seven years, the dual, bus-size Cassini–Huygens probe arrived at the ringed planet Saturn. Cassini went into orbit around Saturn. Huygens detached from Cassini and landed on Saturn's giant moon Titan. Cassini made exciting discoveries, including four new small moons of Saturn.

The magnetometer measured the strength of Saturn's magnetic field.

Huygens spotted huge lakes on Titan. The lakes are not filled with water but the liquid form of the poisonous gases methane and ethane.

The Cassini orbiter circled Saturn.

On the way to Saturn, Cassini–Huygens also studied the largest planet, Jupiter. The probe made new discoveries about the movement of gases in the giant planet's turbulent atmosphere.

Information from the probe took 67 minutes to travel to Earth from Cassini's antenna.

The probe was powered by radioisotope thermal generators (RTGs).

The smaller Huygens probe being carried by Cassini.

Powerful radar and antenna

Instruments were protected from micro-meteorites and temperature extremes by multi-layer insulation.

Huygens landed by parachute on the pebbly surface of Titan, Saturn's largest moon.

NEW HORIZONS

The most distant target of any space mission so far is the dwarf planet Pluto. The full-bed-size New Horizons took off in 2006 on an immense nine-year, 3-billion-mile (5-billion-km) journey. It should reach Pluto and its large moon Charon in 2015. No craft has ever visited Pluto before.

Artist's impression of New Horizons.

EARTH DEFENSE

Asteroids are chunks of rock orbiting the Sun. Some are larger than cities, but in the darkness of space they can be difficult to spot. One day we might detect one on a collision course with Earth. Will there be anything we can do to save our planet?

Asteroid damage to Earth depends on the rock's size, speed, and angle. At a shallow angle it might bounce off the atmosphere. Any impact would cause a gigantic explosion triggering worldwide earthquakes, tsunamis (massive waves), and volcanic eruptions.

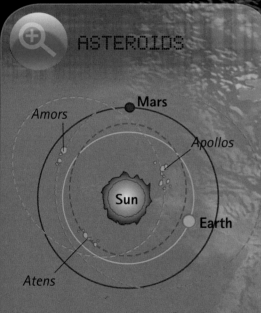

ASTEROIDS

Mars

Amors

Apollos

Sun

Earth

Atens

Most asteroids orbit the Sun far away from Earth, between Mars and Jupiter. However, near-Earth asteroids (NEAs) are much closer. While the Amors asteroids lie outside Earth's orbit, the Atens and Apollos asteroids cross it. The latter pose the greatest threat. The largest Apollo is Sisyphus at 6 miles (10 km) across.

< 212 >

LINKS < 194 MISSION CONTROL 196 SPACE SHUTTLE 206 RETURN MISSIONS

At 20 miles (33 km) long, the Amors asteroid Eros is the second-largest NEA. In 2001, the NEAR Shoemaker probe landed on it. In 2012, Eros will be within 16 million miles (26 million km) of Earth.

BIG BANGS

An asteroid or comet heading toward Earth should be spotted years in advance. If a collision looks likely, one idea is to send a craft carrying a large nuclear bomb to blow it apart. However, some pieces might still reach Earth and cause massive destruction. Another idea is for several nuclear bombs to be exploded near the asteroid, one after the other, gradually knocking it off course without blowing it to bits.

DAWN set off in 2007 toward the asteroid belt between Mars and Jupiter. It should orbit and photograph the largest asteroid Vesta (left) in 2011, then fly on to the even larger dwarf planet Ceres (right) three years later.

DON QUIJOTE MISSION

The European Space Agency plans to launch Don Quijote, a two-craft mission, in 2011. Sancho will travel to a nearby "test" asteroid, but not one that threatens Earth, and study it in detail. The second craft, Hidalgo, will then smash into the asteroid to alter its course. Sancho will monitor the results and radio them back to Earth.

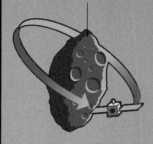

Sancho studies an asteroid 980–1,700 feet (300-600 m) across.

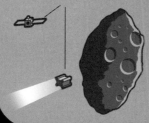

Sancho moves away as Hidalgo crashes into the asteroid.

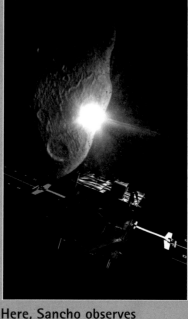

Here, Sancho observes Hidalgo's impact to see if the asteroid changes course.

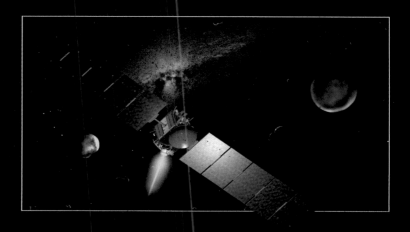

FUTURE SPACE

Although unmanned probes can carry out amazing trips, they are not as smart or adaptable as real astronauts. Plans are now in place to return humans to the Moon, and send a manned mission to Mars.

Propulsion system fueled by propellants are contained in spherical, pressurized, titanium tanks.

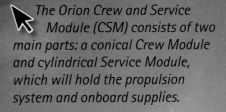

The Orion Crew and Service Module (CSM) consists of two main parts: a conical Crew Module and cylindrical Service Module, which will hold the propulsion system and onboard supplies.

ION THRUSTERS

Most space rockets are very heavy and burn up a lot of fuel very fast. Really long journeys will need more advanced engines or drives. An ion thruster uses electrically charged atoms or molecules for propulsion. While it gives less thrust than a liquid-fuel rocket, making it unsuitable for launching a vehicle into orbit, it is much smaller and can carry enough fuel to last several years.

An ion engine being tested.

The Orion Crew Module will hold 4–6 crew members and will be reusable.

MOON BASE

Since 1969, 12 humans have walked on the Moon, the last in 1972. There are plans to return in about 2020 with mission *Orion 17.* On arrival, part of the Orion craft will remain in the Moon's orbit while the astronauts touch down in a "habitation module." This tiny "hotel" room will form the first part of a future Moon base. The trip is designed to last three weeks.

MARS MISSION

To go to Mars and back, astronauts would need enough food, air, and other supplies to last more than a year. A manned mission is planned for the 2020s, using launch rockets to take sections of a large Mars craft into Earth orbit. The craft would have its own rockets to launch it out of Earth's orbit, a Mars orbiter, a lander, and a living module.

The Mars lander will have a liftoff stage (left) and a living module (right).

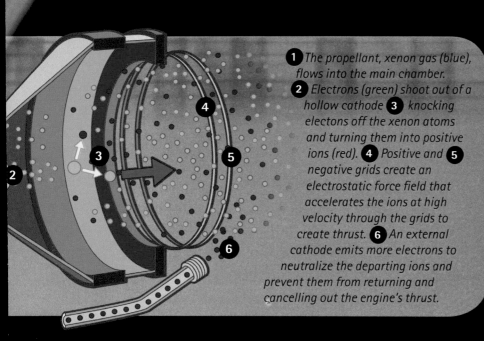

1 *The propellant, xenon gas (blue), flows into the main chamber.* 2 *Electrons (green) shoot out of a hollow cathode* 3 *knocking electons off the xenon atoms and turning them into positive ions (red).* 4 *Positive and* 5 *negative grids create an electrostatic force field that accelerates the ions at high velocity through the grids to create thrust.* 6 *An external cathode emits more electrons to neutralize the departing ions and prevent them from returning and cancelling out the engine's thrust.*

Terraforming, "Earth-shaping," is the process of modifying the atmosphere of a planet or moon in order to make it habitable for humans. One day it may be possible to terraform Mars.

GLOSSARY

Accelerometer A device that senses how much something speeds up, slows down, and makes other movements.

Active medium The substance that forms the main part of a laser. It can be a solid, such as a crystal of ruby, or a gas, such as carbon dioxide.

Aerogel A very light, foamlike substance.

Alternator A type of generator that turns the energy of movement into electricity.

Altimeter A device that uses changes in air pressure to measure height or altitude (usually above sea level) in an aircraft.

Analog Recording information using smoothly varying patterns of electricity, height, or some other quantity.

Atomic clock A clock that uses the movements or vibrations of atoms to detect passing time with incredible accuracy.

Atoms The smallest parts of ordinary matter.

Barcode A pattern of lines and spaces that identifies an object and carries data about it.

Biometric Measuring living things, especially the body and its parts.

Booster An engine or machine that gives added power for a brief time—for example, when a space rocket takes off.

Capacitor A component that stores a certain amount of electricity (an electrical charge), ready to release it when needed.

Central processing unit A microchip that is the main "brain" of an electronic device.

Charge-coupled device A microchip that turns colors and patterns of light rays into digital electronic signals.

Circuit board A flat board with metal wires or strips connecting components, such as microchips and resistors.

Combustion Burning or catching fire, and giving out heat and light.

Composite materials Materials that contain a combination of substances, such as fiberglass and plastic.

Communications satellite A satellite that sends and receives information ranging from TV channels to secret government orders.

Continuously variable transmission When a vehicle has just one gear that makes it speed up faster as the throttle is opened.

Cyclonic motion Swirling or spiraling movements, such as in a hurricane-like storm.

Defibrillator A device that shocks the heart out of rapid, unorganized beats (fibrillation) and back into a regular rhythm.

Digital Using numbers, usually the 0s and 1s of the binary system, to represent data.

Digital recording Recording or storing data in digital form, as binary codes of 0s and 1s.

Diode An electronic component with two electrodes that usually lets electricity flow only one way.

Doppler effect When waves, such as sound waves, are squashed together or stretched apart due to the movement of their source.

Dwarf planet A body in space that is very large, but it is too small to be considered a true planet.

Electrode A metal contact or terminal, usually with a positive or negative charge.

Electron A tiny part of an atom, with a negative electrical charge.

EVA Extra vehicular activity or "space walk," when an astronaut goes outside the craft.

Fiberglass A light and strong material made of thin strands of glass or glasslike substance set into plastic or resin.

Flash memory A microchip designed to hold large amounts of data.

Fuel cell A device that uses a fuel, usually hydrogen gas, to make electricity.

Gamma rays Invisible waves of combined electrical and magnetic energy that are shorter than X-rays.

Generator A device that produces electricity, usually from the energy of movement.

Global warming A rise in temperature across the world caused by adding gases to the air that trap more of the sun's heat.

GPS The Global Positioning System, which uses satellites orbiting the Earth to pinpoint a person's position.

Gravity The pulling or attracting force possessed by all objects.

Gyroscope A fast-spinning device that can detect the movements of things linked to it or keep them steady.

Headset A helmetlike device that shows pictures and produces sounds for the wearer.

Horsepower A measure of power—that is, the rate of doing work or using energy.

Immune system The body's self-defense system, based on blood cells that attack invading germs.

Impeller A small fan or propeller in a tube.

In vitro "In glass," usually something done in laboratory equipment.

Infrared Invisible waves of electrical and magnetic energy that are shorter than microwaves but longer than light rays.

Inoculation Putting a substance into a particular place—for example, a vaccine into the body.

Interferometry Comparing and adding together waves, such as light waves, to find out information, such as how long they are.

Laser High-intensity light or other radiation.

Light-emitting diode A device that gives off light when electricity passes through it in a certain direction.

Magnesium A lightweight, shiny metal that burns fiercely.

Magnet An object with magnetic forces that attract iron and attract or repel other magnets.

Microbes Living organisms too small to see except with a microscope.

Microchip A small slice or wafer ("chip") of silicon bearing hundreds or thousands of electronic devices.

Microwaves Invisible waves of combined electrical and magnetic energy that are shorter than radio waves but longer than infrared.

Motion sensor A device that detects movements and produces electrical signals.

Node A main part of a network, such as the Internet, which receives and sends data.

Nuclear fission Splitting apart nuclei (the central parts of atoms) to release energy.

Nuclear fusion Joining nuclei (the central parts of atoms) to release energy.

Optical fiber A thin, flexible rod of special glass or plastic that carries flashes of laser light representing information.

Orbit To go around in a circle or elliptical (oval) path.

Pairing When electronic devices send information to each other to make a communication link.

Payload The cargo or goods carried, for example, by a space rocket.

Photon A tiny package or piece of light energy.

Photovoltaic Changing light energy into electricity.

Pixel One tiny dot of an overall image.

Powerband The range in which an engine's turning speed (revolutions per minute) produces the most power.

< 218 >

Propellant The fuel in a rocket engine.

Prosthesis An artificial human body part.

Radar Sending out microwaves and measuring the time it takes for them to reflect back from distant objects to find those objects' position and size.

Radio waves Invisible waves of combined electrical and magnetic energy that are longer than microwaves.

Radioisotope An unstable atom that is radioactive and gives off radiation energy.

Receiver A device that detects radio waves.

Regulator A device that controls the amount, speed, or pressure of a substance.

Router A central device that handles data coming and going between computers, other electronic devices, and Internet connections.

Satellite One object that goes around another, usually used to refer to man-made craft going around the Earth.

Scalpel A sharp, surgical cutting blade.

Scanner A device that copies a two- or three-dimensional image, line by line or layer by layer.

Silicon A chemical substance used for microchips.

Skin suit A very tight-fitting body suit made of thin material.

Synthetic material A man-made or artificial substance, not a natural one.

Telemetry Sending measurements over a distance, such as by wires or radio waves.

Titanium A very light, strong, expensive metal, often mixed with other substances in metal alloys or composite materials.

Touch screen A display screen that detects and responds to physical contact.

Transceiver A transmitter-receiver that both sends out and receives information, usually as radio waves or microwaves.

Transponder A device that sends out information according to the information it receives, often in the form of radio waves.

Valve A device that allows a substance to flow in one direction but not the other way.

Voiceprint A visual display of the sound waves of a particular person's voice.

Watt A measure of power—that is, the rate of doing work or using energy.

X-rays Invisible waves of electrical and magnetic energy that are shorter than ultraviolet rays but longer than gamma rays.

< 223 >

ACKNOWLEDGMENTS

All artwork supplied by The Apple Agency Ltd. (apple.co.uk)

Photo credits:
b – bottom, t – top, c – center, l – left, r – right

Front cover: tl Nintendo, tm Kawasaki, tr Wikipedia, c Wikipedia/Matt Britt, bl Michele Westmorland/Corbis, br Wow Wee Toys
Back cover: tl TOSHIYUKI AIZAWA/Reuters/Corbis, tr Softdesign, b Northrop Corporation
Front jacket flap Dreamstime.com/Rafa Irusta
Back jacket flap Kawasaki

8tl Nintendo, 8bl Ed Simkins 9 Monte Cristo, 10tl Ed Simkins 10c Dreamstime.com/Andrea Leone, 11t SwimP3, 11b Klipsch iGroove 11r Chinavision, 12bl Microsoft, 12c Microsoft, 13c Nintendo, 13r Nintendo, 14bl Nintendo, 14c Nintendo, 14–15 Nintendo, 15r Nintendo, 16–17 Cannon 16b Dreamstime.com/Ljupco Smokovski, 16bc Wikipedia, 17r Cannon, 17b Wikipedia, 18l Dreamstime.com/Ghubonamin, 18–19 JVC, 19br Dreamstime.com/Pryzmat, 20t Dreamstime.com 20–21 Dreamstime.com/Bucky_za, 21t Dreamstime.com/Pavel Losevsky, 21b Dreamstime.com, 22cl Dreamstime.com, 22c Charles O'Rear/CORBIS, 23 Dreamstime.com, 24–25 Dreamstime.com/Steve Mitchell, 25tr uslöser/zefa/Corbis, 26l Monte Cristo, 26–27 Monte Cristo, 27t Monte Cristo, 28l Dreamstime.com/Ron Chapple, 28–29 Dreamstime.com, 29t Dreamstime.com/Liguan Guo, 30c Wikipedia, 30b Wikipedia, 31t Screenhire Ltd, 31c Wikipedia, 31b Wikipedia, 32c Noah K. Murray/Star Ledger/Corbis 32 Lester Lefkowitz/CORBIS 33b Dreamstime.com/Rafael Ramirez Lee, 34b David Butow/CORBIS SABA 34l Blackberry, 34b Logitech, 35 Wikipedia/Matt Britt, 36c Wikipedia, 36–37 Samsung, 37r Dreamstime.com/Claudio Rossol, 37c Dreamstime.com, 38c Wikipedia, 38–39 Sony, 39t Schlegelmilch/Corbis 39b Dreamstime.com/Rick Hoffart, 40c Jose Luis Pelaez, Inc./CORBIS 40–41 Logitech, 41t SOHO, 41b Dreamstime.com/Andresr, 42b Artiga Photo/Corbis, 42–43 Blackberry, 43t Dreamstime.com/Jamalludin Bin Abu Seman Abu Seman, 44b Steve Prezant/Corbis, 44c Dreamstime.com/Dmitriy Aseev, 44–45 Dreamstime.com/Stephen Coburn, 45b Dreamstime.com/David Brimm, 46b Dreamstime.com/Rafael Ramirez Lee, 47t Dreamstime.com/Nikolai Sorokin, 47b Dreamstime.com/Aleksandar Jocic, 48b image100/Corbis, 48–49 Dreamstime.com/Doctor_Bass, 49t Wikipedia, 49b TOSHIYUKI AIZAWA/Reuters/Corbis, 50b Dreamstime.com, 50–51 Roberts, 52b Adam Nieman, 52bc Dreamstime.com/Rosmizan Abu Seman, 52c Dreamstime.com/Rafa Irusta, 53t Swiss Army Knife, 53b NASA, 54t Wikipedia, 54tr Dreamstime.com/Brian Macentire, 54b Dreamstime.com, 55 Wikipedia/Matt Britt, 56b Wikipedia, 56–57 7E Communications Ltd, 58bl Yves Gellie/Corbis, 58 ESA, 59t NASA, 60b Piercy Conner Ltd, 60t Bright handle, 61t Wow Wee Toys, 61b Dyson, 62c Wikipedia, 62–63 ZedFactory, 63t Edifice/CORBIS, 63b Dreamstime.com, 64c Wikipedia, 64b Wikipedia, 64–65 iStock/Michael Kemter, 65b iStock, 66tl Reuters/Corbis, 66–67 Reuters/Corbis, 67b Reuters/Corbis 68l, 68t, 68b Home, Micro Compact Home, 69t, 68c, 68b Piercy Conner Ltd, 70l LG, 70r CC-Concepts Ltd, 71t Gorenje, 71b Ernestomeda, 72l Neorest, 72–73 Neorrest, 73c Brighthandle. 73r Dornbracht, 73b iStock/Alexandra Draghici, 75 Wikipedia, 76l Dyson, 76c Dyson, 77c Reuters/CORBIS, 77b Viatek, 78t Nokia, 78b Dreamstime.com, 79c Dreamstime.com, 79b Wikipedia, 78t Dreamstime.com/Omar Ariff Kamarul Ariffin, 80b Dreamstime.com, 79b SSEI KATO/Reuters/Corbis, 80b L. Clarke/CORBIS 80tl Dreamstime.com, 82c iRobot, 83t iRobot, 83bl, 83br Wikipedia, 84, 85t Wow Wee Toys, 85r Honda, 86b Lockheed, 86t Kawasaki, 97b Wikipedia, 87t Bugatti, 88–89, 88b, 89t Bugatti, 89b McLaren F1, 90l, 90br, 90–91, 91t Segway, 91b Wikipedia, 92l Wikipedia, 92–93 moodboard/Corbis, 93t Kawasaki, 93b Wikipedia, 94–95 Honda, 95tr OSHIYUKI AIZAWA/Reuters/Corbis, 95tc Wikipedia, 95b Honda, 96 Kawasaki, 97c Dreamstime.com/Daniel Boiteau, 97b Wikipedia, 98c Car Culture/Corbis, 98b Wikipedia, 98–99 Dreamstime.com, 100b, 100–101, 101t, 101b P1 Power boat, 102–103 Chris McLaughlin/CORBIS, 102b Woods Hole Oceanographic Institution, 103t Stephen Frink/zefa/Corbis, 103b Wikipedia, 104t, 104–105, 105t Wikipedia, 106b Dreamstime.com/Kameel4u, 106c Wikipedia, 106r Magellan, 107b Garmin Forerunner, 108c, 108t, 109t, 109b, 109br Gulfstream, 110c Northrop Corporation, 111c Lockheed, 111b Wikipedia 112t Adidas, 112b Dreamstime.com, 113bl Adidas, 113r Kawasaki, 114 Adidas, 114b Jerry Lampen/Reuters/Corbis, 115t Paul Miller/epa/Corbis, 115b Gore-Tex, 116b, 116t, 117c, 117b Adidas, 117tr Leo Mason/Corbis, 118l moodboard/Corbis, 118b Polar Foot Pod, 118–119, 119t, 119b Adidas, 120l, 120b Suunto, 120–121 Suunto, 121b Suunto, 122b Wikipedia, 122c Dreamstime.com 122–123 Anne-Marie Sorvin/Icon SMI/Corbis, 123t, 123c Forcefield Body Armour, 123b Dreamstime.com, 124b, 124t Hawkeye, 125b Tim de Waele/Corbis, 125r Seiko/Reuters/Corbis, 126–127 Burton Snowboards, 126br Dreamstime.com, 127b Dreamstime.com, 128b iStock, 128–129 Dreamstime.com, 129c Oliver Furrer/Brand X/Corbis, 130b Michele Westmorland/Corbis 131–131 Dreamstime.com, 131t iStock, 131b Reuters/Corbis, 132–133 Suunto, 133bl Wikipedia, 133br Suunto, 134l, 134b, 135t, 135b Kawasaki, 136–137 Gary L. Tong/NewSport/Corbis, 136t Schlegelmilch/Corbis, 137t Schlegelmilch/Corbis, 138l Pixland/Corbis, 138–139 iStock, 139 Dreamstime.com, 140l Pixland/Corbis, 140c Dreamstime.com/Trout55 141t Mediscan/Corbis, 141b Dreamstime.com/Millan, 142b Dreamstime.com/Sebastian Kaulitzki, 142–143 iStock, 143r MedicalRF.com/Corbis, 143b Matthias Kulka/zefa/Corbis, 144b Achim Scheidemann/dpa/Corbis, 144–145 Digital Art/Corbis, 145bl Wikipedia, 145br iStock, 145t Wikipedia, 146l Dreamstime.com, 146b Dreamstime.com, 146–147 Dreamstime.com, 147r MURPHY-WHITFIELD/Image Point FR/Corbis, 148t Swiss Army Knife, 148bl iStock, 148br Tool Logic, 149t Doug Wilson/CORBIS 149b David Spurdens/Corbis, 150–151 Dreamstime.com/Pawel Nawrot, 150bl iStock, 151t Thinkstock/Corbis, 151b Lester Lefkowitz/CORBIS,152c Brooks Kraft/Sygma/Corbis, 152–153 Dreamstime.com, 153b iStock, 154br, 154t Advanced Bionics, 155t iStock, 156c iStock, 156t Jason Reed/Reuters/Corbis, 156–157 Alessandro Di Meo/epa/Corbis 157b Eric Preau/Sygma/Corbis, 158b, 158c, 159t, 159b EndoWrist, 160–161 Dreamstime.com/Billyfoto, 160t Dreamstime.com, 161l Wikipedia, 162l Wikipedia, 162b Baci/CORBIS, 163b Tony Savino/Corbis, 163t Dreamstime.com 164l KUKA, 164b Wikipedia, 165t John Deere, 165c 3D Systems, 165b iStock, 166l Frederic Pitchal/Sygma/Corbis, 166r Wikipedia, 167l, 167c, 167r KUKA, 168t Wikipedia, 168b , 167t Softdesign, 167b , 170c Charles O'Rear/CORBIS, 172c Dreamstime.com/Dainis Derics, 172–173 Wikipedia, 173t Wikipedia, 173c Dreamstime.com/Keith Frith, 173r, 173b Wikipedia, 174t, 174b, 174br ZCorporation, 175t 3D Systems, 175b ZCorporations, 176l Dreamstime.com/Stephen Sweet, 176b Wikipedia, 176–177 Dreamstime.com, 177t Wikipedia, 177b Robert Llewellyn/Corbis, 178r, 178–179, 179r R. E. Palmer Birmingham University, 179tc Dreamstime.com/Vitaly Valua, 179t Dreamstime.com/Yurii Gorul'ko, 179b Dreamstime.com, 180c William Whitehurst/CORBIS, 180b David Pollack/CORBIS, 180br Wikipedia, 181b TFL, 182l, 182–183, 183t, 183b John Deere, 184tr Bob Daemmrich/Corbis, 184tl iStock, 184–185 iStock, 185bl Dreamstime.com/Kamil Sobócki 185br Greg Smith/CORBIS, 186c Dreamstime.com/Jean Schweitzer, 186t, 186–187 Wikipedia, 188l NASA, 188–189 JET Culham, 189 ITER, 190t, 191t, 191b NASA, 192t, 192b, 192–193, 193t, 193b European Southern Observatory, 194c NASA, 194–195 Wikipedia, 195t ESA, 195b Dreamstime.com, 196t ESA, 196–197 NASA, 197b NASA, 198c Wikipedia 198b ESA 198–199 Wikipedia, 200b Richard Baker/Corbis, 200c Jim Sugar/CORBIS 201c NASA, 202–203, 203b, 203r NASA, 204c, 204r NASA, 205 SOHO, 205c SOHO, 206l, 206tr, 206br NASA, 207c JAXA, 207t, 207b NASA, 208–209 NASA, 208bl ESA, 208br NASA, 209r, 209b NASA, 210b, 210–211, 211r, 211b NASA, 212–213 Sanford/Agliolo/CORBIS, 213t NASA, 213c ESA, 213b NASA, 214b Wikipedia, 214–215 NASA, 215c ESA, 215b NASA.

< 224 >